BEGINNINGS

BEGINNINGS

EDITED BY PATRICIA DREIER

A READER'S DIGEST/C.R. GIBSON BOOK
Published by The C.R. Gibson Company
Norwalk, Connecticut 06856

The acknowledgments that appear on pages 94-95 are hereby
made a part of this copyright page.

A Reader's Digest/C.R. Gibson book published by arrangement
with The Reader's Digest Association, Inc., Pleasantville,
N.Y. 10570.

Printed in the United States of America.

ISBN 0-8378-1807-9

Table of Contents

Introduction

THE BEGINNING OF ADVENTURE AND EXCITEMENT
One Step To Excitement   *Elizabeth Starr Hill* 10
Dare To Make Mistakes   *Beth Day* 14
Take That Chance   *Frank Harvey* 17
"Dig Into The World"   *Alan Alda* 20
The Grammar Of Life   *William Wallace Rose* 25
Words Of Wisdom From Dr. Seuss   *Theodore Seuss Geisel* .. 26

THE BEGINNING OF NEW STRENGTH
The Magic Of Enthusiasm   *Michael Drury* 28
Secrets Of The Soaring Spirit   *Hilton Gregory* 32
The Awesome Power To Be Ourselves   *Ardis Whitman* 36
Make Your Dreams Come True   *Norman Vincent Peale* 41
Seven Secrets Of Peak Performance   *Morton Hunt* 45

THE BEGINNING OF A RICHER LIFE
Overtaken By Joy   *Ardis Whitman* 50
Do Clouds Sleep?   *Ronald Rood* 56
Now . . . While There's Time   *Ed Bartley* 60
Perfect Moment   *Gladys Bell* 65
A Moment Can Last Forever   *Graham Porter* 67
The Night The Stars Fell   *Arthur Gordon* 69

THE BEGINNING OF SELF-DISCOVERY
The Adventure Of Being Alone   *Eric Sloane* 74
Meaning For My Days   *Joan Mills* 77
"I Wanted To Do It All"   *Virginia Morell* 81
A Walk Across America   *Peter Jenkins* 86

Introduction

Life is a kaleidoscope of changes and beginnings. . .some minor, others overwhelming. Retiring from work, graduating from school, starting a new job or moving to a new home—we stand on the threshold of a new life, a fresh start. We may hesitate on the threshold afraid to take that very first step. Yet with that step we can receive wisdom, growth and enrichment.

BEGINNINGS helps us to see the bridges rather than the pitfalls as we discover the thrill of living a new life. To begin again is to meet each day with the enthusiasm of a child, to accept each minute as an unrepeatable miracle, to sense the magic and excitement in everything around us.

Beginning is rarely easy. After all, old habits and problems are more familiar (and maybe even more comfortable) than new ones. To begin again we must find the inner strength to learn new patterns, and see with new vision.

And it is a great adventure. Change may be frightening but it's also exhilarating. Look ahead. There is a bright new world awaiting you right outside your own front door.

THE BEGINNING OF ADVENTURE AND EXCITEMENT

ONE STEP
TO EXCITEMENT

The rewards of seeing bridges rather than pitfalls.

One morning my husband called from work unexpectedly. His voice was exuberant: "Honey, we have a big choice to make. I've been offered an eight-month assignment in the London office. If I take the job, you and the children would fly over with me next week. What do you think?"

For a minute I was too stunned to answer. All I could see was a formidable array of problems. How could I ever pack, close the house and leave *next week*? Suppose our two small children did not adjust to English schools? I was stammering the list of difficulties, when, suddenly a memory came to me of another day and another choice. I was 16 years old, a city girl visiting my Aunt Alice in the country. One day we took a walk. It was hot, the dirt road was rough underfoot. I clung to the shade, worrying about sunburn.

We came to a stream half-screened by beeches, with a glimpse of meadow on the other side. Impulsively Aunt Alice said, "How pleasant that meadow looks! Let's wade across and see what it's like over there!"

I shrank back, complaining that we would cut our feet on the stones. And there would be little shade in the meadow; my nose would get red and peel. We had walked a long way, this would make an even longer trip home, we would be tired tomorrow. . . .

Exasperated, Aunt Alice cut in. "What a misuse of imagination! You're picturing pitfalls where bridges ought to be!"

The brusque words startled me into silence. She pulled off

her shoes and stockings and plunged into the stream. I followed. On the other side, we pushed past a branch of beech and came upon a field of daffodils, hundreds of them, just as in the Wordsworth poem—a vast orchestra of golden trumpets sounding the hosanna of spring. Did my nose peel? Did I hurt my feet? I don't remember. But I'll never forget those glorious daffodils.

With that moment again vivid in my mind, I spoke to my husband on the phone with more courage. "Well, if we do go, what a wonderful experience it might be!"

"I think so, too," he answered quickly. "If we want adventure, let's take just one step toward it."

The next week, we flew to eight marvelous months in London. We're glad that we didn't turn our backs on adventure.

So often we act as though some ironclad rule prevented us from setting foot on unfamiliar ground! We tend to repeat the same old things in the same old ways, to be wary of trying anything new. Yet just one step from our well-beaten paths of habit can, on occasion, take us to the land beyond the rainbow.

Sometimes it's difficult to believe how short a distance we need to travel to put ourselves on a desired path. As a little girl, I was sick a lot and didn't go to school regularly until I was almost nine. I still remember clearly that first awful day. The other children seemed to know everything—games, lessons, one another. How I yearned to be like them, and how unlikely it seemed that I ever would be!

Silent and frightened, I hid in corners. When recess came, I stood alone at the edge of the playground. After a while, my teacher came over and commented gently, "It seems hard, at first, to get to be one of the gang. But if you'll . . ."

Before she could go on, I burst out weeping. I told her that I knew she wanted me to join in games and talk, but I couldn't possibly. I didn't know how to skip rope; the rules of hopscotch were Greek to me—and so on.

When at last I ran down, the teacher said mildly, "I was only going to suggest that you go over to someone and say hello."

Nothing complicated. And I managed to do it. And, of course, it worked. One step leads us to another and then to the next, and so we travel distances we never would have believed possible.

I have a friend whose mother was a wonderful gardener, justly famed for her beautiful and inventive landscaping. The mother had always dreamed of having enough land for an all-white garden. Finally she managed to buy the property she wanted—and died three weeks later.

Her daughter, who inherited the property, was not noted for her green thumb. But she had been inspired by her mother's dream and decided that somehow she would create the white garden. As she took her small daughter on a tour of the bare, unplanted grounds, however, a dreadful sense of inadequacy oppressed her. Half laughing, half despairing, she asked, "Stacy, if you wanted to make the most beautiful garden in the world here, how would you begin?"

The child thought for a moment, then replied, "I'd buy a package of seeds."

My friend did exactly that. Now, three years later, the white garden is a glowing testament to a daughter's love and a child's common sense. The child had seen the first step, not the first pitfall.

My father, who loved art, was confined to his home by illness for the last years of his life. Realizing that he would never again be able to visit museums or explore galleries, he refused even to discuss art. All of us in the family grieved, but we could not seem to help.

One day Mother showed him an advertisement for inexpensive reproductions of paintings. "Why not send for one of these?" she suggested.

At first my father dismissed the idea, with a dozen objections. Later we saw him rereading the advertisement. Finally, he mailed off an order. When it arrived, he spent several hours in a half-grumbling, half-appreciative examination of the pictures, ending with a grudging, "Interesting, anyway. Wonder what other prints this outfit has?"

He sent for a catalogue. Before long, prints, art books, etchings were flooding into the house. My father was a busy man again, sitting on the couch with a card table before him, sorting, cataloguing and studying.

When Father died, he left a fascinating collection. Even more, he left shining proof of the fact that God rings us all around with chances for happiness. If one path becomes closed to us, we can simply step off to another—unless we are afraid to try.

The roads to adventure are never distant. There are many of them, and they all begin at our own front door—just one step away.

ELIZABETH STARR HILL

Life does not consist either of wallowing in the past or of peering anxiously at the future. It is good to appreciate that life is now—this day—this hour—and is probably the only experience of the kind one is to have. As the doctor said to the woman who complained that she did not like the night air: "Madam, during certain hours of the twenty-four, night air is the only air there is."

CHARLES MACOMB FLANDRAU

DARE TO MAKE MISTAKES

Recently, I went with a friend, who had opened her own decorating shop, to call on a prospective client—a very rich, but crusty, old woman. "I doubt I'll get the job," my friend confided. "I know she's already turned down every other shop in town!"

When we had surveyed the room, and my friend gave her estimate, the old woman suddenly fixed her with a sharp stare and said, "Have you ever made a mistake?"

"Why—of course!" my friend replied, startled.

"Fine," the old woman said. "You can take the job. I didn't want to fool with someone who hadn't had a chance to benefit from previous mistakes."

Mistakes are not only an acceptable part of life; they are essential to a full life. Without the intelligent use of our mistakes, we would never go on to master any skill.

George Bernard Shaw said, "A man learns to skate by staggering about, making a fool of himself. Indeed, he progresses in all things by resolutely making a fool of himself." But many of us, terrified by the possibility of failure or ridicule, deprive ourselves of pleasures, adventures and just plain fun by being too concerned with what people will think. Shattering as it may be to our egos, the fact is that most people never observe us as closely and critically as we believe.

An editor friend, who seems quite self-assured, once confessed that for years he had watched others ski, but was held back from trying it himself by the thought that he might appear ludicrous. Finally, when he was approaching middle age, it occurred to him that if he didn't ski now, he never would. "Of course, I look ridiculous out there," he admits cheerfully. "But I couldn't care less. I'm doing something I've always wanted to do, and I'm having a grand time!" Other skiers, far from being critical, admire his zest for learning.

Let's face it, in any new thing you attempt, there will always be someone better at it than you are. But the pursuit of a full and rewarding life is not competitive; it is an individual search for happiness. Sunday painters, for example, are not aiming at an exhibition at the Museum of Modern Art; they are merely satisfying their own artistic desires. Impossible standards of perfection bleed us of our peace of mind. The sooner we accept the comforting fact that we are less than perfect, the sooner we can get on with our personal and professional goals.

The greatest successes in life are those fortunate few who have learned to take title unflinchingly to their mistakes as well as their accomplishments. Such individuals waste no emotion on vain regrets when they do err. John D. Rockefeller, Jr., recalled about his father: "Never did I hear him utter a single word of regret. With him, what had happened could not be helped. How to repair damage, how to rebuild, how to turn apparent defeat into victory—this was his immediate concern throughout life."

Sometimes parents, to encourage top performance, set standards that are impossibly high. "They tell children so often that it will be a great disappointment if they do not measure up," says Bonaro W. Overstreet, in *Understanding Fear*, "that they virtually force those children into an exaggerated fear of failure, and into an exaggerated self-dislike when failure occurs."

One of the first things to realize is that accomplishment follows a natural course of trial and error. "We are prone to toss our children the finished products of man's achievements—the radio, the telephone, a lifesaving medicine," pointed out Charles F. Kettering, the automotive inventor. "But we do this without telling them about the painful processes by which these miracles came into being. We should emphasize that virtually nothing comes out right the first time."

Many major achievements have resulted from adventurous mistakes which became stepping-stones to success. Young Winston Churchill made so many outrageous blunders that he was damned by the press for his "lack of discretion and judgment." Fortunately, he did not allow that indictment to curtail his activities.

To admit mistakes takes a sense of humor, and this wisdom, too frequently, does not come until late in life. But, in the words of Emerson: "Finish each day and be done with it. You have done what you could. Some blunders and absurdities no doubt crept in; forget them as soon as you can. Tomorrow is a new day; begin it well and serenely, and with too high a spirit to be cumbered with your old nonsense."

BETH DAY

TAKE THAT CHANCE!

I was getting ready for the "mud dive." You went down 50 feet in the icy water in front of the U.S. Naval School, then located in Bayonne, N.J., and sank deep into the mud—and if you didn't panic, you could complete the rest of the rigorous training to become a diver.

"You really don't *have* to make this dive," Chief Petty Officer Dan Crawford told me as I sat on the stool in my deep-sea suit. "We can fill you in on how it is."

"Bolt the helmet on, Chief," I replied, "before I change my mind."

Six months earlier, I'd been sitting on a padded chair in an advertising agency with a steady salary and an expense account. Then the little painless lesion on my cheek was tested and found to be malignant. In my terror of cancer, I found resolve. "Christine," I said to my wife, "all my life I've wanted to try my hand at free-lance writing. Now I'm going to give it a whirl—while I still can."

I quit my job, and we put down $5000—all our savings—on a huge, decrepit old stone farmhouse in northern New Jersey. Out back was an old chicken coop which, to my enchanted eye, had the makings of a writer's studio. I moved in an old captain's chair and my typewriter, and was ready for business. This assignment—about the initial descent of a Navy diving student as diving was then taught—was one of my first big ones.

I backed down into the water and, keeping a tight grip on the line, let myself sink into the gloomy depths. Ear pains began at once—and became excruciating. When my diving glove slipped on the slimy line, I began to sink fast, and one of my heavy diving boots jammed in a piling. Red wheels of panic revved up in my head. "Bring me up!" I yelled into the helmet microphone.

Dan Crawford was chuckling when he lifted off the helmet. Something had been collecting in the back of my throat. I spat it out—bright-red blood. "You broke some blood vessels in your Eustachian tubes," Crawford said. "It happens all the time. But you did okay—got to 40 feet."

I sold the story, and was able to pay a lot of back bills. But, most important, I had finally put into action the working philosophy that I had adopted for my new career: pick the most demanding mission, go through it yourself, then tell what happened. Henry David Thoreau wrote: "The cost of a thing is the amount of what I will call life which is required to be exchanged for it, immediately or in the long run." To me, this translates: when a chance is offered, *take it*.

I've been doing this now for 34 years, and my chicken-coop studio is cluttered with mementos—all of them earned by Thoreau's kind of coin. There is the blue-woolen diver's cap that I wore for the mud dive. Those handcuffs on the bookcase were used when I was writing a story about a kidnapped boy. I wrote it nine times. Flat as stale soda. Then I asked Christine to handcuff, gag and blindfold me, and drive me over rough back roads just the way the boy had been carried off. She drove so fast that I was black and blue from bouncing around. At one point, I thought I was going to swallow the gag. I was weak with relief when we stopped. But the exercise paid off. The kidnap sequence wrote itself: the story was published and, later, anthologized.

One memento in my chicken-coop collection has nothing to do with writing. It is a "Lucky Sea Bean," the "nut" of a tree that grows along the Amazon. These nuts fall into the river, float out into the ocean and are eventually washed up in places like Daytona Beach, where I found mine. I value it because it reminds me of the retired philosophy professor who gave me the best tip on chance-taking. On a rough day when the surf was making the dunes shake, he would wade out into the fury, duck under a big roller and swim out to sea. One morning I could stand it no longer. I asked him why.

"I've wanted to do it all my life," he replied. "But big waves always terrified me. Then I weighed the dangers and decided I would *have* to try. I waded out, watched until one of those monsters towered up like a cliff; then I ducked under. When I surfaced behind that wave, I was king of the world!"

His eyes twinkled. "No man can hope to control his destiny. The best he can hope for is to control himself—*one single act at a time*. Those acts are like bricks in a wall. A wall made of such bricks is a man's character."

I believe this because, shortly afterward, I put it to the test. Driving up our road one winter day, I saw fire billowing out of the chicken coop. My first thought was for the one and only copy of a long, nearly completed manuscript. I skidded into the driveway, left the car on the dead run, and a moment later was staring into a wall of flames between me and the desk, where the manuscript lay in a plastic box. I took a deep breath, squinted my eyes, lunged through the fire, grabbed the box, and got out—all in one breath. Only then did I feel the pain in my hands from the nearly molten plastic. The burn scars that I still carry probably make up the best brick I'll ever put in my wall.

I find I keep coming back to Thoreau's words concerning the true cost of a thing—anything. I do not advocate rashness: look before you leap. But when I see a person, young or old, rich or poor, who has a realizable dream for which he is willing to exchange a piece of his life, I know that person is building toward the highest goal. He is rising to a new level of being, using his precious will to become stronger, braver, maybe even kinder and wiser.

FRANK HARVEY

"DIG INTO THE WORLD"

In words that sparkle with wit, this commencement address deals with such matters as courage, laughter, work, chutzpah and love. The time: May 1980. The speaker: the star of the popular television program "M*A*S*H." The audience: his daughter and her classmates at an Eastern college.

The best things said come last. People will talk for hours saying nothing much and then linger at the door with words that come with a rush from the heart.

We are all gathered at a doorway today. We linger there with our hand on the knob chattering away like Polonius to Laertes. Now remember, *Neither a borrower nor a lender be . . .* and don't forget, *This above all: To thine own self be true . . .*

But the very best things said often slip out completely unheralded, preceded by, "Oh, by the way." In real life, when Polonius had finished giving all that fatherly advice to his son—who probably wasn't paying much attention anyway—he must have said, "Oh, by the way, if you get into any trouble, don't forget you can always call me at the office."

As we stand in the doorway today, these are my parting words to my daughter. There are so many things I want to tell you, Eve.

The first thing is: don't be scared. You're being flung into a world that's running about as smoothly as a car with square wheels. It's okay to be uncertain. Adulthood has come upon you and you're not all that sure you're ready for it. I think that sometimes I'm not ready for adulthood either—yours *or* mine.

The day before yesterday you were a baby. I was afraid to hold you because you seemed so fragile. Yesterday, all I could feel was helplessness when you broke your nine-year-old arm. Only this morning you were a teen-ager. As I get older, the only thing that speeds up is time. But if time is a thief, time also leaves something in exchange: experience. And with experience, at least in your own work you will be sure.

Love your work. If you always put your heart into everything you do, you really can't lose. Whether you wind up making a lot of money or not, you will have had a wonderful time, and no one will ever be able to take that away from you.

I want to squeeze things great and small into this lingering good-by. I want to tell you to keep laughing. You gurgle when you laugh. Be sure to gurgle three times a day for your own well-being. And if you can get other people to join you in your laughter, you may help keep this shaky boat afloat. When people are laughing, they're generally not killing one another.

I have this helpless urge to pass on maxims to you, things that will see you through. But even the Golden Rule doesn't seem adequate to pass on to a daughter. There should be something added to it. Here's my Golden Rule for a tarnished age: Be fair with others, but then keep after them until they're fair with you.

It's a complex world. I hope you'll learn to make distinctions. A peach is not its fuzz, a toad is not its warts, a person is not his or her crankiness. If we can make distinctions, we can be tolerant, and we can get to the heart of our problems instead of wrestling endlessly with their gross exteriors.

Once you make a habit of making distinctions, you'll begin challenging your own assumptions. Your assumptions are your windows on the world. Scrub them off every once in a while, or the light won't come in. If you challenge your own, you won't be so quick to accept the unchallenged assumptions of others. You'll be a lot less likely to be caught up in bias or prejudice, or be influenced by people who ask you to hand over your brains, your soul or money because they have everything all figured out for you.

Be as smart as you can, but remember that it's always better to be wise than to be smart. And don't be upset that it takes a long, long time to find wisdom. Like a rare virus, wisdom tends to break out at unexpected times, and it's mostly people with compassion and understanding who are susceptible to it.

The door is inching a little closer toward the latch and I still haven't said it. Let me dig a little deeper. Life is absurd and meaningless—unless *you* bring meaning to it, unless *you* make something of it. It is up to us to create our own existence.

No matter how loving or loved we are, it eventually occurs to most of us that deep down inside, we're all alone. When the moment comes for you to wrestle with that cold loneliness, which is every person's private monster, I want you to face the thing. I want you to see it for what it is and win.

When I was in college, 25 years ago, the philosophy of existentialism was very popular. We all talked about nothingness; but we moved into a world of effort and endeavor. Now no one much talks about nothingness; but the world itself is filled with it.

Whenever that sense of absurdity hits you, I want you to be ready. It will have a hard time getting hold of you if you're already in motion. You can use the skills of your profession and other skills you have learned here, dig into the world and push it into better shape.

For one thing, you can try to clean the air and water. Or you can try to make the justice system work, too. You can bring the day a little closer when the rich and privileged have to live by the same standards as the poor and the outcast.

You can try to find out why people of every country and religion have at one time or another found it so easy to make other people suffer. You can try to stop the next war now, *before* it starts, to keep old men from sending children away to die.

And while you're doing all of that, remember that every right you have as a woman was won for you by women fighting hard. There are little girls being born right now who won't even have the same rights you do unless you act to maintain and extend the range of equality. The nourishing stew of civilized life doesn't keep bubbling on its own. Put something back in the pot for the people in line behind you.

There's plenty to keep you busy for the rest of your life. I can't promise this will ever completely reduce that sense of absurdity, but it may get it down to a manageable level. It will allow you once in a while to bask in the feeling that, all in all, things do seem to be moving forward.

I can see your brow knitting in that way that I love. That crinkle between your eyebrows that signals your doubt and your skepticism. Why—on a day of such excitement and hope— should I be talking of absurdity and nothingness? Because I want you to focus that hope and level that excitement into coherent rays that will strike like a laser at the targets of our discontent.

I want you to be potent; to do good when you can, and to hold your wit and your intelligence like a shield against other people's wantonness. And above all, to laugh and enjoy yourself in a life of your own choosing and in a world of your own making. I want you to be strong and aggressive and tough and resilient and full of feeling. I want you to be everything that's you, deep at the center of your being.

I want you to have chutzpah. Nothing important was ever accomplished without chutzpah. Columbus had chutzpah. The signers of the Declaration of Independence had chutzpah. Laugh at yourself, but don't ever aim your doubt at yourself. Be bold. When you embark for strange places, don't leave any of yourself safely on shore. Have the nerve to go into unexplored territory.

Be brave enough to live life creatively. The creative is the place where no one else has ever been. You have to leave the city of your comfort and go into the wilderness of your intuition. You can't get there by bus, only by hard work and risk and by not quite knowing what you're doing. What you'll discover will be wonderful. What you'll discover will be yourself.

Well, those are my parting words as today's door closes softly between us. So long, be happy . . . .

Oh, by the way, I love you.

ALAN ALDA

Many years ago Rudyard Kipling made a commencement address at McGill University in Montreal. He said one striking thing which deserves to be kept in remembrance. He was warning the students against an overconcern for money, or position, or glory. He said, "Someday you will meet a man who cares for none of these things. Then you will know how poor you are."

DR. HALFORD E. LUCCOCK

THE
GRAMMAR
OF LIFE

William DeWitt Hyde, when president of Bowdoin College, advised his students:

Get your grammar right and all other needful things will fall to you.

Live in the active voice, not the passive. Think more about what you make happen than about what happens to you.

Live in the indicative mood, rather than the subjunctive. Be concerned with things as they are, rather than as they might be.

Live in the present tense, facing the duty at hand without regret for the past or worry over the future.

Live in the first person, criticizing yourself rather than finding fault with others.

Live in the singular number, caring more for the approval of your own conscience than for the applause of the crowd.

And if you want a verb to conjugate, you cannot do better than to take the verb "to love."

WILLIAM WALLACE ROSE

WORDS OF WISDOM FROM DR. SEUSS

Children's-books author Theodor Seuss Geisel—better known as Dr. Seuss—gave the following address at Lake Forest College in Illinois.

It seems to be behooven upon me to bring forth Great Words of Wisdom to this graduating class as it leaves these cloistered halls to enter the Outside World. Fortunately, my wisdom is in very short supply, and I have managed to condense everything I know into this epic poem consisting of 14 lines:

My Uncle Terwilliger on the Art of Eating Popovers

My uncle ordered popovers
from the restaurant's bill of fare.
And, when they were served, he regarded them
with a penetrating stare . . .
Then he spoke great Words of Wisdom
as he sat there on that chair:
"To eat these things," said my uncle,
"You must exercise great care.
You may swallow down what's solid . . .
BUT . . . you must spit out the air!"

And . . . as you partake of the world's bill of fare,
that's darned good advice to follow.
Do a lot of spitting out the hot air.
And be careful what you swallow.

THE BEGINNING OF NEW STRENGTH

THE MAGIC OF ENTHUSIASM

Nobody is born bored. In the morning of our lives a caterpillar is an astonishment and a pink-iced cake a marvel. But somewhere en route to adulthood we lose our enthusiasm, not because we have grown wise and sad, but because we misconceive it to be callow.

True adult enthusiasm is not puppy-dog eagerness for every new smell and sound and blade of grass, but rather the original endowment grown up—tempered and shaped by experience, judgment, humor. The word enthusiasm comes from *entheos*—the god within—and means basically to be inspired or possessed by the god, or, if you like, by God. It is the open secret, as commonplace and tireless as sunlight, that gives joy and purpose to all our days, if only we don't despise it.

The taproot of enthusiasm is learning. Learning makes us a child again in relation to the new thing, but it also means admitting that we don't already know. When I was in college there was a country lad who was an expert square dancer but wished to learn what he called "round dancing." The other boys laughed at him, but the girls didn't. He would say, "I'd ask you to dance, but I don't know how. Will you teach me? I like music. I like pretty girls, too." We taught him; we scrambled for the privilege.

A woman in her mid-60's took her first plane trip and for half an hour was miserably uneasy. "I finally realized," she said afterward, "that I wasn't afraid of flying. I was afraid of not knowing how to act in a plane. I was wild to ask questions, but I first had to admit my greenhorn standing. Once over that hurdle, I got along fine. And I learned some fascinating things

about planes. You see, the air resembles a fluid, like water. . . ."
And she was off, the quintessence of enthusiasm.

Enthusiasm is sustained by the free play of our faculties. Too often, for example, our vision is exercised as a tool, too rarely as a joy. When crossing the street, we see a car coming and we go back to the curb. We need such practical information to survive, but its usefulness ought not to eclipse awareness of that world beyond, where a yellow taxi on a rain-black pavement is transportation, yes, but also a streak of color across a gray day and a reason to have eyes.

Early one spring evening I walked down a busy New York street with a man who had been working fiercely hard. Suddenly he stopped and said, "I hear a cricket." Horns blew, feet hurried by, and that man's mind was groggy with problems— yet he heard a cricket. We hunted until we found him, scraping his legs at the edge of a grating, and we smiled and went on oddly comforted, reminded of our own ability to perceive and receive a world. I learned then that enthusiasm is partly willing attention, a turning aside to see, instead of hunching up inside like the affronted snail. Without enthusiasm, we are blind and deaf and only half-know our world.

A little girl I know is a fledgling marine biologist who spends her allowance on specimens. One day I asked her if this passion wasn't depriving her of other important things, after-school treats and movies. "I suppose so," she said. "But if I can't have both, I'll take biology."

She had already learned that without purpose there is no lasting delight. It's hard to be enthusiastic and aimless. I have learned again and again that when I travel to a new city as a tourist I often enjoy it without gaining any real desire to go back; if I go on business, with places I must see and people I must talk with, I touch some deeper pulse of that city and am aroused to know it better.

There comes a time in nearly every life when purpose fails and fundamental enthusiasm quits, taking with it to some extent our very will to live. This dulling of the radiance can come about abruptly, because of a crisis, or gradually, from the abrasion of daily living. It can happen when a long-held job is snatched away; or on that morning when you find yourself so-and-so-many years old without having done a tenth of the things you'd planned.

The temptation is strong to give up. But this is the one moment above all others to hang on. The human mind is lazy and loves not to be disturbed. But some tough sinew of it—that very portion that is capable of enthusiasm—doesn't run to fat; it stretches thin and snaps us back.

One of the most exhilarating women I know was hit by a series of blows, culminating in the loss of a young son. For two or three years she was indifferent to everything. After a gap of some time we met, and I was much comforted to find her luster restored. "Day after day," she said, "I had to *make* myself go about my daily work. Everything was flat. Then one day I saw a couple quarreling on the street, so young, and so in love. I found myself understanding them—I can't tell you how much. I talked with a refugee woman who told me about her lost family in Europe, and I understood, truly understood. I found myself with a new heart and a new enthusiasm. I feel that understanding is the one thing that can save the world. If it took grief to teach me, at least I've learned that."

There is no magic formula that can cloak us with gladness in living. It comes from willingness to find one's own way— indeed, enthusiasm *is* that willingness. At times this involves acceptance of things as they are; at others it means daring to change things. A favorite story in our family concerns a fore-bear who was a quick-draw Nevada newspaper editor in the days of the Comstock Lode. One day he saw a young woman struggling to back and turn her horse and carriage. He strode over, unhitched the horse, picked up the gig with the girl in it, and turned it about. Then he backed the horse into the shafts, re-hitched him, raised his hat to the speechless young woman and went his way. Later, of course, he married her.

That man lived all his life at an audacious clip. I doubt it even occurred to *him* that people sometimes must bow to circumstances. But every field of endeavor has its hazards, and sometimes it is not one's business to change them.

At a dinner I heard a Broadway producer expound on his trade. He spoke of a mulish writer, an unheated rehearsal theater, the incredibly childish behavior of some actors—and someone asked him why he put up with it. He shrugged. "That's the way it is," he said, summing up several centuries of show business. "I can't *bother* about it; I've got a show to get on."

Somewhere between wanting to make the world over and wanting to hide from it is a balance that permits intelligent, adult enthusiasm. This god within becomes the art without, and we no longer beg to know what life means: we furnish the meaning by being.

MICHAEL DRURY

SECRETS OF THE SOARING SPIRIT

Earthlings we may be, but we know that there is some of the sky in us.

It came in the mail with a collection of bills. Hundreds of copies of it must have gone out to residents of the suburb I live in, announcing that the local historical society wanted volunteer researchers. I let the letter slide into the wastebasket.

Then, something made me fetch it out again. Within a week, I was on a study committee. Soon I was writing a paper, delivering a speech, meeting new friends. But the most remarkable thing is what the experience did for my outlook and feelings. I found that my spirit soared, borne aloft by the new interest.

About that time, I read a sketch of Ralph Waldo Emerson. I learned that as a sickly youth he had been given up by the doctors. He went south to die—"yet still his spirit soared." The words leaped out at me. Anyone who has read Emerson even cursorily knows the multiplicity of his interests, and can guess that the exhilaration of new discoveries from day to day lifted him above defeat and ill health. He lived to be 78.

There are those such as Emerson whose talent and disposition enable them to rise above adversity or the humdrum of existence. Always mounting above petty resentments, their talk moves up from palaver about people to principles and ideas. You can't get these people down, because their spirits are elsewhere, elevated and renewed by interests. They perceive others' views by rising above their own.

Fortunately for us, soaring spirits have characteristics we can study. Here are some specific traits I have observed:

They don't make reaching out a chore. Soaring spirits instinctively know that the road to new interests is the *natural* route of fascination and delight; they do not drearily *drive* themselves to self-improvement. Some of us grimly jog instead of enjoying long walks, attend encounter sessions instead of trying to communicate with our marriage partners. A leisurely approach that trusts spontaneous curiosity permits our faculties to soar.

They exploit their moments of inspiration. Even greatness has only intervals of glory. Periods of transcendence may be brief. In such periods, the artist, animated by what is known as the "divine afflatus," operates far above ordinary abilities. He knows the importance of these moments, and uses them while others waste them.

We have all enjoyed moments of unaccountable good feeling: work does itself; we feel strong and confident; problems shrink. We must learn to take the current when it serves. What we need to notice is that these moments are usually associated with new things that interest us.

They rise with their natural thermals of interest. My friend Bob Buck, a retired international airline pilot who loves to soar, took me up in a sailplane and, without the power of a motor, we remained aloft for hours. The sky seems empty and motionless, but Bob knows that it is alive with capricious currents and invisible elevators—most of them going up.

You soar in a sailplane by finding what the skypilots call thermals—immense columns of warm air rising from the earth. At their minimum, thermals may support the sailplane; at their maximum, they lift it high in moments of shuddering excitement. The skilled pilot gets the best out of every thermal he finds, circling and rising in its broad embrace. When it plays out, he glides gently downward until he feels the lift of another thermal. If he doesn't find any, he glides gently downward until he feels the lift of another thermal. If he doesn't find any, he glides back to earth, trailing his experience behind him.

Everyone knows that there are around us every day thermals of interest. A penetrating book or conversation with a new friend can propel us to maneuvering heights. Once we are up, we have the cooperation of a skyful of ideas.

They find inspiration in others. People often soar by means of the interests of other people as well as their own. I learned the principle when my younger son directed a vacation jaunt from plan to finish. To none of the places he chose would I have gone without the tutelage of his enthusiasm. There was a newness of perspective in his interests, so different from my own. I tarried over new territory, and was renewed.

Everyone you meet has some interest you don't have. The judicious use of ears will suffice to acquire it. Here is a chance to get above yourself by letting the sincerity and intensity of another's concerns buoy you.

They follow the current wherever it may lead. In youth, before we get trammeled by requirements, we learn how far a new interest can take us. I remember hearing a college lad talking about one subject that "won't take any time at all. Unless," he added, "I get interested."

There are regions of culture most likely to lift the spirit. Philosophy, art and religion are three areas in which man transcends himself. I have found the landscape of language worth a try. Words have great warmth—and a height that arises out of their history. And there are at least 450,000 possible thermals in the biggest dictionary!

Most of us will never be what Sir Walter Scott described as the soaring and ardent spirit for which the earth seems too narrow. Yet we all have what Shakespeare called "immortal longings" in us. I remember the fable of the eaglet stolen from its nest and chained to a stake. The story has it that the captive, fed and befriended, survived and accepted its lot until one day an eagle appeared in the distant sky. Each day the eagle came closer, circling lower and lower, until at last it touched the captive with its wing. It was this act that made the bird on the ground tug with such might that it pulled up the stake and took off.

Whatever the grubbiness of our lot as earthlings may be, we know that there is some of the sky in us. We may not be able to pull up stakes, but there will be times when we will be touched by wings and want to soar.

HILTON GREGORY

The best cosmetic in the world is an active mind that is always finding something new.

MARY MEEK ATKESON

THE AWESOME POWER TO BE OURSELVES

One afternoon, when I was a little girl, the teacher announced that there would be no school the next day because the old man who lived in the turreted mansion had died. I was puzzled. Many people died. Why close the school for this man?

I asked Stuart, who was in the eighth grade and usually knew everything. "He owned the factory, didn't he?" Stuart said, amazed at my ignorance. "That's about as powerful as you can get around here."

Isn't this how many of us think of power—the richest man in town, the man who can control others?

But power has many guises. My father was a kind and gentle country minister in Nova Scotia. He had neither money nor fame. No one, I am sure, was ever afraid of him. When he was 64 years old, he received a letter from a church official in one of his old parishes. "We hear that you will soon be retiring," the man wrote. "Would you come and settle here? We feel that we'd be a better community and better neighbors for having a man whose life is so genuine living among us."

Imagine changing a community just by being oneself. That is power.

I think of a homely little man in Athens more than 2000 years ago who died because he asked dangerous questions. His audiences were very small; yet there is no literate person in the world today who has not heard of Socrates. I think of St. Francis of Assisi, who gave up a pampered life to live in poverty while comforting the poor and the sick, and of Mohandas Gandhi, who freed his people from the most powerful empire of his time, without any force except what he called "truth force."

What do these individuals have in common? They all spoke and acted as themselves, resolutely standing up for what they believed. They had the inner purity of people true to their ideals. They were "authentic."

Many critics nowadays decry the "be yourself" philosophy as leading to selfishness. But *authenticity* doesn't do this. It proceeds from the center of a person's life, but is not self-centered. It sets a glowing example for others and moves them to action. It is available to all of us.

Authenticity makes each person's life count by restoring *power* to the individual. To be oneself is a natural, human and universal power, which brings with it a cornucopia of blessings.

Today, best-sellers are written on the powers of assertiveness and manipulation. But in our society, the assertive manipulators often do not win. Many of our institutions are headed by authentic people, who rise because others are drawn to them, admire them, imitate their example. Here is an upright business leader who has risen to the top over others who are more clever. Why? His associates might say he is "fairer," or that he has a longer "vision," but it is more than that. The man possesses an inner strength; he radiates confidence. Instinctively honest, he never weakens his moral authority by a dishonest compromise. This honesty is one prime attribute of authentic people. Others include:

A sense of direction. Authentic people recognize the direction in which their lives are meant to go. When Albert Schweitzer, the great missionary doctor, was a boy, a friend proposed that they go up in the hills and kill birds. Albert was reluctant, but, afraid of being laughed at, he went along. They arrived at a tree in which a flock of birds was singing; the boys put stones in their catapults. Then the church bells began to ring, mingling music with the birdsong. For Albert, it was a voice from heaven. He shooed the birds away and went home. From that day on, reverence for life was more important to him than the fear of being laughed at. His priorities were clear.

Self-generated energy. Fatigue is a common symptom of people who have suppressed what is truly themselves. We are often tired from the effort not to be ourselves. We are actors trying to impress other people. That's hard work.

By contrast, the authentic person does not dissipate energy in contradictions. His self-honesty reduces internal conflicts, and he feels alive, exhilarated. His energy is turned on by doing what matters to him. He does not dissipate energy on conflicts or deceits.

The power of example. The authentic person also mobilizes the energies of others, by inspiring them. Just by being himself, he makes a statement about what is to be done.

During the French occupation of the Saar in the 1920s, when German feelings were running high against reported excesses by black colonial troops, Roland Hayes, the great black singer, faced a noisy and hostile audience in Berlin. For almost ten minutes, he stood quietly but resolutely by the piano, waiting for the hissing to cease. Then he signaled his accompanist and began to sing softly Schubert's "Du bist die Ruh" ("Thou Art Peace"). With the first notes of the song, a silence fell on the angry crowd. As Hayes continued to sing, his artistry transcended the hostility and a profound communion between singer and audience took place.

The power of self-love. A person who respects and values himself is much more likely to be able to do the same for others. When we are not sure who we are, we are uneasy. We try to find out what the other person would like us to say before we speak, would like us to do before we act. Authentic people, on the other hand, are *there*, not only for themselves but for others. No energies are wasted in protecting a shaky ego.

The power of the spirit. No one can summon spiritual power just by wanting to. But it seems to come often to those most centered on the deep self where discovery begins. I think of Martin Luther King, Jr., marching between the clubs and the baying dogs to Selma, Ala., and electrifying a huge audience in the Washington Mall. It was impossible to be with him for any length of time without realizing that the spirit was the spring from which he took his life's responses. Few of us can be great leaders, but any person who is true to himself enhances his access to this power of the spirit.

Striving for authenticity is not easy. It's a lifetime endeavor, and nobody ever makes it all the way. It is a becoming rather than an ending, something we learn day by day. Here are some ways to begin:

Pay attention to what is going on in your life, inwardly and outwardly. Keep a journal to see how you change over time and to discover what muffled longings are being expressed. Few of us are so monolithic that we don't harbor conflicts within ourselves. Admit them. Listen to the dialogue within and record it in your journal. As May Sarton wrote in *World of Light,* "Everything free from falsehood is strength."

Accept the idea that nothing is wrong with being different from other people. The truth is, all of us are different, and we are meant to be. "Each one of us," wrote philosopher Paul Weiss, "is a unique being confronting the rest of the world in a unique fashion." Seek out your deepest convictions and stand by them, live by them.

Spend time with yourself. Solitude is at the heart of self-knowledge, because it is when we are alone that we learn to distinguish between the false and the true, the trivial and the important. "Solitude," said Nietzsche, "makes us tougher toward ourselves and tenderer toward others."

As with the splitting of the atom, the opening of the self gives us access to a hidden power. Authenticity is a sensitizing and blessed power. It comes with feeling at home with oneself, and therefore at home in the universe. It is the greatest power in the world—the power to be ourselves.

ARDIS WHITMAN

Dr. Eric Berne, author of the bestselling Games People Play, *is hardly a conventional psychiatrist. "Life is simple," he insists. "All you have to do about problems is make decisions. But people want certainty. You cannot make decisions with certainty. All you can do is compute likelihoods. People don't like that."*

Losers spend their lives thinking about what they're going to do. Winners, on the other hand, are not afraid to savor the present, to "unpack their books" and "listen to the birds sing." Losers say "but" and "if only." Winners are enlightened people who grow rich, healthy, happy, strong, wise and brave using just three words in life: Yes, No, and Wow! "Wow!" is to express the healthy childlike wonder in all of us.

JACK FINCHER

MAKE <u>YOUR</u> DREAMS COME TRUE!

As a youngster I had some pretty negative self-images. My father and mother were both unusually able, strong-minded, outspoken individuals. And I felt I'd never measure up to them, or to their ambitions for me. Another thing bothered me: I was a "preacher's kid." I had the feeling that people expected me to be a goody-goody, that adults would condemn me if I wasn't and my friends would despise me if I was.

This self-image of inadequacy might have gone on indefinitely had it not been for something a professor said to me during my sophomore year in college. One day after I had made a miserable showing, he told me to wait after class. "How long are you going to be bashful like this," he demanded, "a scared rabbit afraid of the sound of your own voice? You'd better change the way you think about yourself, Peale, before it's too late."

I left that classroom angry, resentful, hurt, but most of all frightened because I knew that what the professor had said was true.

I sat down on the steps of the chapel and prayed a deep and desperate prayer: "Please let me see myself not as a scared rabbit but as someone who can do great things in my life because you are giving me strength and confidence."

When I got up, something had changed. The inferiority feelings were not all gone; I still have some of them to this day. But the *image* I had had of myself was changed—and with it the course of my life.

As the years went by, I began using imaging techniques whenever I wanted to achieve a certain goal. Now and then my old feelings of inadequacy would come back to haunt me, but usually I was lucky enough to discover an image of success that was stronger than my image of failure.

I remember a mass meeting one Memorial Day sponsored by the American Legion. Fifty thousand people crowded into Brooklyn's Prospect Park, where the guest of honor was Lt. Col. Theodore Roosevelt, Jr. I had been invited, I thought, merely to open the meeting with a prayer. But when I got there, I found that I was listed on the program as the main speaker.

A wave of panic swept over me. I had no speech prepared. The thought of standing before 50,000 people and disappointing them terrified me. I went to the sponsors of the gathering and told them that I couldn't do it. I wouldn't do it. They would have to find somebody else.

Roosevelt overheard my lamentations. "Son," he said, "stop focusing on failure. You're a minister, aren't you? Here you have a chance to minister to all these grieving mothers. You can tell them how much we love them for the sacrifice they've made. You can tell them how proud this country is of the sons and husbands they lost. So get up there and talk, and I'm going to sit right behind you and visualize you loving these people and helping them and holding them spellbound for the next twenty minutes. I have a picture of this in my mind, and it's so strong that I know it's going to happen!"

So, shamed into it, I tried to do as he said. And his image of my succeeding must have been stronger than mine of failure, because the talk went pretty well. Afterward, Roosevelt said to me, "Now, you see, if you think you can, or somebody who believes in you thinks you can, why, then you can!"

Perhaps the idea of the power of positive thinking was conveyed to me right then and there. But behind that idea, in it and beyond it was the concept of imaging—holding the *image* of yourself succeeding, visualizing it so vividly that when the desired success comes, it seems to be merely echoing a reality that has already existed in your mind.

I remember one time when the imaging process worked in a dramatic fashion. It was a stormy Sunday night in Manhattan. Wind howled around the corners of the skyscrapers, sending sheets of rain mixed with sleet swirling along the streets. I was scheduled to talk, as usual, at the evening service. As my wife, Ruth, and I drove slowly down to Marble Collegiate Church from our home on 84th Street, I became more and more agitated because I was convinced I would be talking to nothing but empty pews.

"This is awful," I said to Ruth. "Terrible. Nobody in his right mind will come out in this weather." I kept on in this negative fashion for block after block. Finally, Ruth could stand it no longer. She pulled the car over to the curb and parked in the drumming rain.

"What's the matter with you?" she demanded. "You're always preaching optimism and positive thinking. Now you're just thinking about yourself and whether or not you'll have a large audience." She pointed at the tall apartment houses around us, gray in the rain, the yellow lights of windows shining dully. "Why don't you think about all the hurting people in these apartment houses? Why don't you visualize them streaming into the church, filling every pew, bringing their needs and their problems, finding solutions? Let's pray about this. Let's ask for the church to be full, not to buttress your pride, but so you have people to help. Let's see it full, and give thanks that it will be full!"

So we held hands and prayed and imaged, visualized. Then we drove on down to the church and—what do you know—we couldn't find a parking space.

We finally found a place two blocks away, walked back two blocks through the rain, and—just as we had imaged it—the church was jammed!

Can it be argued that the church would have been full anyway that night? Of course it can. But who knows how many people who were hesitant about going felt a sudden impulse to go?

Let the skeptics have their doubts. I prefer to believe that ideas do have wings!

Over the years, Ruth and I have studied the principle of

imaging and worked with it, testing it in many demonstrations of actual experience under varied circumstances. We have concluded that this technique is effective in just about all the important areas of living. It is one of the great principles of creative living.

Keep in mind, however, that imaging is not a magic formula that, simply, by some kind of mental trick, brings results. In an amazing way, it does open doors to problem solving and to goal achievement. But once those doors are open there must be discipline, determination, patience and persistence if problems are to be solved or if dreams are to become reality. In this way, you will find, as we have, that what you can image, you can be.

NORMAN VINCENT PEALE

There is a wonderful way to develop the ability to adapt to change. It is a simple drill with a far-reaching effect: do something new and different once each day for a while. Not necessarily anything extremely unusual or startling—it can be merely doing a familiar thing in a different way. If you always put on your left shoe first, try putting on the right one. Walk down a different side of the street from the one you are used to.

This, a psychologist friend told us, forms new pathways in the brain. Then, when next you meet a block in some direction of thinking or action, you will be able to accept it constructively or come up with a way around it which previously might have seemed to lead to a dead end.

Entirely apart from developing the ability to adapt, this discipline is also rewarding and pleasant in the doing and in the new doors that it opens.

JEAN HERSEY

SEVEN SECRETS OF
PEAK PERFORMANCE

In every walk of life, star performers share certain mental skills and habits that anyone can learn.

Two of my classmates in college hoped to have careers in publishing. Each was talented, personable, ambitious. Yet Roger now heads a multimillion-dollar book company while Jack has a dull, modestly paying job editing business directories.

Why has one man flown so much higher than the other? Not because of luck, connections or dedication to work—but simply because Roger is a peak performer and Jack is not.

Charles Garfield, member of the clinical faculty of the University of California, San Francisco and president of the Performance Sciences Institute in Berkley, has studied more than 1500 outstanding achievers in nearly every walk of life. He finds they all have certain traits in common—traits that are not innate but which *can be learned by anyone*.

This doesn't mean that everyone can become a company president or win an Olympic medal. It *does* mean that all of us can learn to make much more of the gifts we have. Here, based on Garfield's research, are seven steps that can lead to peak performance:

1. *Lead a well-rounded life.* High achievers, we often hear, are inevitably "Type A" personalities—hard-driving, obsessed

people who bring work home and labor over it until bedtime. Not so, according to Garfield. "Such people tend to peak early," he says, "then go into a decline or level off. They become addicted to work itself, with much less concern for results."

High performers, in contrast, are willing to work hard—but within strict limits; for them, work is not everything. When Garfield interviewed top executives in ten major industries, he found that they knew how to relax, could leave their work at the office, prized close friends and family life, and spent a healthy amount of time with their children and intimates.

2. *Select a career you care about.* Although he really wanted to edit children's books, my former classmate Jack chose business-directory publishing as a likelier path to a large salary. For 30 years he has dragged himself out of bed five days a week to work at something he doesn't care about—and which has never produced the hoped-for pay. If Jack had done what he really wanted to do, he might—or might not—have made more money. But he almost certainly would have been a happier and more successful human being.

Garfield's data show that high performers choose work they truly prefer, and spend over two-thirds of their working hours doing it and only one-third on disliked chores. They want *internal* satisfaction, not just *external* rewards such as raises, promotions and power. In the end, of course, they often have both. Because they enjoy what they are doing, their work is better and their rewards higher.

3. *Rehearse each challenging task mentally.* Before any difficult or important situation—a board meeting, a public appearance, a key tennis match—most peak performers run through their desired actions in their minds over and over. Famed golfer Jack Nicklaus, for example, never takes a golf shot without first mentally visualizing the precise trajectory of his swing, the flight of the ball, the spot where it lands.

Nearly all of us daydream about important coming events. But idle daydreaming isn't the same as a deliberate mental workout that hones the skills actually used in the activity.

4. *Seek results, not perfection.* Many ambitious and hard-working people are so obsessed with perfection that they turn out little work.

When University of Pennsylvania psychiatrist David D. Burns, author of *Feeling Good: The New Mood Therapy,* tested a major insurance company's top 69 salesmen, he found that those who had perfectionist tendencies earned from $8000 to $10,000 less a year than those who did not. This does not surprise Garfield. High performers, he has found, are almost always free of the compulsion to be perfect. "They don't think of their mistakes as failures," he says. "Instead, they learn from them so they can do better the next time."

5. *Be willing to risk.* Most people stay in what Garfield calls the "comfort zone"—settling for security, even if it means mediocrity and boredom, rather than taking chances. High performers, by contrast, are able to take risks because they carefully consider exactly how they would adjust—how they would salvage the situation—if, in fact, they did fail.

Constructing a "worst-case scenario," as Garfield calls it, allows you to make a rational choice. If you remain immobilized by fear, you have no choice at all.

6. *Don't underestimate your potential.* Most of us think we know our own limits. But much of what we "know" isn't knowledge at all but belief—erroneous, self-limiting belief. "And self-limiting beliefs," says Garfield, "are the biggest obstacle to high-level performance."

For many years everyone "knew" that running a mile in less than four minutes was "impossible." Articles published in journals of physiology "proved" that the human body couldn't do it. Then, in 1954, Roger Bannister broke the four-minute barrier. Within two years ten other athletes had followed suit.

This is not to say there are *no* limits on how fast a human being can run—or on how much weight a person can lift or how well one can do any particular task. The point is: we rarely *really* know what these limits are. Thus too many of us too often set our individual limits far below what we could actually achieve.

High performers, on the other hand, are better able to ignore artificial barriers. They concentrate instead on themselves—on their feelings, on their functioning, on the momentum of their effort—and are therefore freer to achieve at peak levels.

7. *Compete with yourself, not with others.* High performers focus more intently on bettering their own previous efforts than on beating competitors. In fact, worrying about a competitor's abilities—and possible superiority—can often be self-defeating.

Because most high performers are interested in doing the best possible job by their own standards, they tend to be "team players" rather than loners. They recognize that groups can solve certain complicated problems better than individuals and are therefore eager to let other people do part of the work. Loners, often over-concerned about rivals, can't delegate important work or decision-making. Their performance is limited because they must do everything themselves.

Such are the skills of high performers. If you want to make more of your talents—to live up to your full potential—then learn to use them. As Garfield explains, "I'm *not* saying 'Try harder' or 'Why don't you do better?' I *am* saying that you have the power to change your habits of mind and acquire certain skills. And if you choose to do so, you can improve your performance, your productivity and the quality of your whole life."

MORTON HUNT

THE
BEGINNING
OF A
RICHER LIFE

OVERTAKEN BY JOY

To miss the joy is to miss all.

Robert Louis Stevenson

It was a day in late June, gray and depressing, with clouds hanging low. My husband and I were driving to Nova Scotia for a much-needed vacation, both of us more tired than we cared to admit. We traveled glumly, hoping to reach rest and dinner before the rain came. Suddenly, on a lonely stretch of highway flanked by woods, the storm struck. The forest vanished in a great deluge. Cascades of water shut us in, making driving impossible. We pulled off onto the shoulder of the road and stopped.

Then, as though someone had turned off a celestial faucet, it ended. A thin radiance, like a spray of gold, spread out from the clouds, catching the tops of the trees. Every blade of grass was crystalline as the sun flashed on trembling drops. The very road shone. And then a rainbow arched across the sky. But more than that: on our right was a pond, and in the pond was the end of the rainbow! It was as though this arch of living color had been built for us alone. We could hardly speak for awe and joy.

A friend of mine has described a similar experience. She had walked out on a lonely beach at twilight. It was a time of grief for her, and loneliness was what she wanted. Offshore, across the darkening sea, was a single low island. Presently she was aware of a dim light moving on the island, and then came the splash of oars and the scrape of a boat leaving the shore. She made out the outlines of a fishing boat, and in it the figure of a man. He rowed a little way and anchored. My friend told me that, after a while, she felt an intense and glowing sense of oneness with that silent figure. It was as though sea and sky and night and those two solitary human beings were united in a kind of profound identity. "I was overtaken by joy," she said.

Most of us have experienced such lighted moments, when we seem to understand ourselves and the world and, for a single instant, know the loveliness of all living things. But these moments vanish quickly, and we are almost embarrassed to admit that they have ever been, as though in doing so we betray a willingness to believe in what is not true.

However, the late psychologist Abraham Maslow, former chairman of the department of psychology at Brandeis University, embarked some years ago on a study of average, healthy individuals and found that a great many report such experiences—"moments of great awe; moments of the most intense happiness or even rapture, ecstasy or bliss." He has concluded that these experiences are often the expression of buoyant psychological health.

Apparently almost anything may serve as the impetus of such joy—starshine on new snow; a sudden field of daffodils; a moment in marriage when hand reaches out to hand in the realization that this other person speaks as you speak, feels as you feel. Joy may wait, too, just beyond danger when you have been brave enough to face a situation and live it out. Whatever the source, such experiences provide the most memorable moments of human life.

Joy is much more than happiness. It is "exultation of spirit," says the dictionary, "gladness; delight; a state of felicity." Awe and a sense of mystery are part of it; so are the feelings of humility and gratitude. Suddenly we are keenly aware of every living thing—every leaf, every flower, every cloud, the mayfly hovering over the pond, the crow cawing in the treetop. "O world, I cannot hold thee close enough!" cried the poet Edna St. Vincent Millay in such a moment.

Enthralled, we see as we never saw before. The most important thing in these peak experiences, said Professor Maslow, is the feeling of these people that they had really glimpsed "the essence of things, the secret of life, as if veils had been pulled aside."

We see, too, the unity of all things—a dazzling vision of the kinship we all have with one another and with the universal life around us. Suddenly we know who we are and what we are meant to be. All doubts, fears, inhibitions, tensions and weaknesses are left behind. This is our true self and we have found it.

"To miss the joy is to miss all," wrote Robert Louis Stevenson. For these moments of joy are like flowers in the pastureland of living; or like a plow turning up the gasping earth in a dry and weed-bound field. Life grows larger, we draw deeper breaths, doors open softly within us.

The sad thing is that it happens to most of us so rarely. As we grow older, our lives become buried under the pressures of the workaday world.

What we need is the child's spontaneity and wonder of discovery. "To me every hour of the light and dark is a miracle," wrote Walt Whitman.

How can we restore to our lives this eager openness to all the world which is so often the prelude to joy? Sometimes all that is needed is a chance to see an old experience in a new way. I remember one such occasion. I had been working all night on a manuscript. It would not come right, and I felt I could never finish it. But as the clock struck five, the last sentence fell into place and I put down my pen, opened the door and stepped out onto the lawn. The stars were thinning out and the sky in the east had that "light-is-coming" look. A few birds began to sing, tentatively trying out their voices, each seemingly waking the next. The trees, dark shapes on the horizon, began now to take on form and configuration. A streamer of light caught the weeping willow across the street and sharply etched one branch of our birch tree. The sky lightened all along the eastern horizon. More trees appeared, one by one. The great maples lighted with brilliance like candelabra in the dark.

The sun was up! There was a golden blaze behind the dark trees, a quickened freshness in the air. Twig by twig the sun set fire to every branch and leaf. The birds now were singing wildly as though they had just been created by the morning itself; and I, too, felt newly created, so full of joy that it seemed I could not hold it.

Most of us need to learn to break out of the prison of self. For joy comes not only from fusion with nature; it comes from love and creativeness; from insight and discovery and great emotion.

Perhaps joy is most likely to come when we forget ourselves in service, or in the pursuit of a great dream. Handel wrote his *Messiah* in a little more than three weeks. Tradition has it that he worked morning, noon and night, hardly touching the food set before him. When he had finished Part Two, which contains the "Hallelujah Chorus," he cried, "I did think I did see all heaven before me and the great God Himself!"

Most of all, joy may come when we do not run from life—from its sorrows, its struggles and its hopes. When life's transiency and frailty are omnipresent, what we have grows sweeter. As G. K. Chesterton said, "The way to love anything is to realize that it might be lost."

I remember finding myself seated beside an old gentleman on a train some years ago. He sat quietly looking out of the window. His eyes searched each leaf, each cloud, the lines of passing houses, the upturned faces of children watching the train go by.

"It *is* beautiful, isn't it?" I ventured at last, intrigued by his absorption.

"Yes," he said, and no more for a moment. Then he smiled and waved a hand at a passing hay wagon. "See," he said. "Hay going to the barn." And he made it sound as though there could be no greater event in all the world than a wagonload of hay on its way to the mow.

He saw the unspoken question in my face. "You think it's strange," he said, "that just a hay wagon means so much. But you see last week the doctor told me that I have only three months to live. Ever since, everything has looked so beautiful, so important to me. You can't imagine how beautiful! I feel as if I had been asleep and had only just waked up."

Perhaps we are more likely to experience a moment of joy if we can admit that there is more to life than we have yet fathomed; if we can acknowledge a world greater than our own.

In my own life there was a moment of this special exaltation. En route by plane to the Midwest, we were flying at a high altitude, and a continent of shining clouds spread beneath us. Often, before and since, I have watched these radiant towers and hillocks of cloud go by. But this time the scene was haunted by a strange joy so penetrating that the plane seemed not to be there. I thought of myself as living and walking in a land like that, and I, who am the most gregarious of humans, knew in a flash of deep illumination that there was in the universe a light, a stuff, a tissue, a substance in company with which one could never be lonely. The experience left the compelling certainty that we dwell safely in a universe far more personal, far more human, far more tender than we are.

What if these moments of joy are given us to reveal that this is the way we are meant to live? What if the clarity of joy is the way we should be seeing all the time? To many people, it seems almost wicked to feel this radiance in a world threatened as ours is. But most generations have known uncertainty and challenge and peril. The more grievous the world, the more we need to remember the luminous beauty at the center of life. Our moments of joy are proof that at the heart of darkness an unquenchable light shines.

ARDIS WHITMAN

I believe that only one person in a thousand knows the trick of really living in the present. Most of us spend 59 minutes an hour living in the past, with regret for lost joys, or shame for things badly done (both utterly useless and weakening)—or in a future which we either long for or dread. Yet the past is gone beyond prayer, and every minute you spend in the vain effort to anticipate the future is a moment lost. There is only one world, the world pressing against you at this minute. There is only one minute in which you are alive, this minute—here and now. The only way to live is by accepting each minute as an unrepeatable miracle. Which is exactly what it is—a miracle and unrepeatable.

STORM JAMESON

DO CLOUDS SLEEP?

A naturalist gains refreshing new glimpses of the world through the eyes of children.

I owe a big debt to a man and a boy from Rutland in my adopted state of Vermont. The two were a father-son combination from a Scout troop who materialized at my door one afternoon. "We're supposed to get a speaker for our annual Dads' Night banquet," the boy said. "Would you come and talk to us?"

"Well, thanks," I said. "But what would you want me to talk about?"

"Oh, anything. You know, animals or camping or wildlife. Something from your new book, maybe."

That was my first speaking engagement. I don't remember, now, what I told them besides some camping stories. All I know is that it was the best talk I ever gave. Best for me, at least. It opened the door to a new world. Here, I discovered, was a chance to get away from the typewriter and meet people—especially little people. Visiting with the Scouts was an education. After that first talk, it was hard to stop me.

One visit to a second grade will long remain in my memory. I had shown slides of a volcano in Hawaii pouring molten rock into the sea. Where the lava met the ocean, a pillar of steam rose a mile into the air. You could almost hear it roar. Afterward, I passed around a chunk of lava. When it had been through two dozen hands, a youngster came forward with the lava, his eyes wide. "Mr. Rood," he said, carefully cradling the material, "it's still warm!"

To be able to make a lump of lava come to life, so to speak, is all the success I need. Something of what I feel struck a chord in a young boy's life—and his imagination one in mine.

Seldom do I make a school visit without gaining refreshing new glimpses of the world as seen through youthful eyes. As Prof. William Lyon Phelps told my college graduating class, "Although I've been in school almost constantly since I was three, there's not a first-grader alive who cannot tell me *something*."

It's fun to get letters from kids, too, even when they lay it on the line. A youth I had known for several years did just that: "Our teacher says we should write to someone important, and if not someone important, someone interesting, and I thought of you. Do you know anybody?"

In a burst of (I hope) enthusiasm, another boy wrote: "My friends and I have desided on a word for your talk. And that word is grate."

As a speaker, and before that a researcher for encyclopedia services for readers, I find that children's curiosity gives me continual new perspectives on nature:

"My teacher asked me to write to you to see if you could answer us a question. The question is, 'If gravity pulls down, why do we grow up?' "

"Does a cat have nine lives? Ours just died and it was the first time. Why is this?"

"What would one do if he was lost in the Okefenokee Swamp? Please rush reply, as I need it immediately."

"What do cows think about when they're hitched in the stanchion all night?"

"I would like to know how the snow crystals form their buetyful shapes."

The mother of a four-year-old, at a loss for an answer, wanted me to tell her daughter if clouds ever sleep.

"Does a frog bump his bottom when he jumps?"

Original research—such as getting a frog and finding out what bumps when it jumps—was beyond my responsibility. However, the frog question was too fascinating to leave alone. My wife, Peg, and I both happen to be interested in water creatures, so we took a number of flash photos of jumping frogs. We learned that those gangly-legged critters land in all sorts of ways—front-feet first, hind-feet first, belly-whackers, nose dives. Apparently grace is not one of the strong points of your average frog.

The enthusiasm of youngsters is fun enough when I'm visiting a classroom. Take them outside, and the pleasure is doubled. They readily touch and feel and smell a fuzzy plant or a fluffy seedpod. Interesting facts about plants and animals are painlessly absorbed: the way a butter-and-egg plant yawns when you squeeze it, or the galloping gait of a squirrel that results in its hind feet landing in front of its forefeet so the tracks seem as if it were running backward.

In July and August I often visit summer camps. One day I was a guest at a camp in Plymouth, Vt. "The nature trail starts off by the edge of the garden," director Ken Webb said, with a wave of his hand. "The kids'll show you where it goes from there."

I started out with a dozen campers. Aided by their sharp eyes and keen senses, we discovered the hollow-tree home of a litter of flying squirrels and solemnly contemplated the shelving ledge that served as a chipmunk's front door. We found a "nest" the size of a bathtub where a deer had bedded down. We made balloons from the thick leaves of the live-forever plant, and carved whistles out of the twigs of a willow.

At lunch, Ken and I were talking about the morning's walk. He asked if I had any suggestions for improvement of the trail. "Not really," I told him. "The only thing I might suggest is to have a trail go in a loop so you don't have to backtrack to get home again."

"But it *is* in a loop, Ron—less than half a mile."

Of course. Those campers and I had become so enthralled

with what we found that in three hours we covered only about 500 yards of woodland path—and then turned back.

It reminded me of a comment once made by the renowned naturalist Louis Agassiz, when asked what he had done during the summer. "Oh," said Agassiz, "I spent it traveling. I got half-way across my back yard."

RONALD ROOD

There is more to be felt and learned about the world and one-self in half an hour's walk up a country hillside than in a flight around the earth at twice the speed of sound.

CHARLES YOST

NOW . . .
WHILE THERE'S TIME

A father and his infant daughter travel different roads. But there are also lovely moments when they walk together.

"Missy," I called to my wife, "did you smear Vaseline on the top of my desk?"

"No, honey. Meghan probably did." Just like that. Calm. As I feared, she had missed the carefully honed, double-edged irony of the question. I *knew* she hadn't put it there. The question was rhetorical; its only function was to make clear to her that she hadn't done her job: defend my desk against the aggressor.

I abandoned the conversation. I would deal with Meghan, our 22-month-old daughter, later.

All that was yesterday. Today I sit here at that same rolltop desk, which I salvaged from a friend's attic two years ago, and stare at the blank sheet inserted in the typewriter. I wait patiently for ideas to come to me, exam questions on Herman Melville for a test I will give my English students tomorrow. My wife is off to a reunion somewhere, but I am not alone. Our two children keep me company. Ten-month-old Edward cooperates to some degree; he spends most of his day poring over a seemingly endless array of cards, tags, assorted pieces of paper, and a Sears, Roebuck catalogue which he tears apart page by page. Occasionally he leans out and flails madly at the piano, which he can just reach.

But it is Meghan whose plans have been destined from all eternity to clash with mine today.

She follows a daily routine that is both time-consuming and

challenging. It includes certain basic tasks: Watching the "grop." (That would be the fish; I cannot explain the derivation of the word beyond that.) Sweeping the rug in her room and crib. (Yes, Meghan sweeps her crib.) Sitting for a few minutes on the bottom shelf of the bookcase to determine whether or not she still fits there. (She fit yesterday and the prospects look good for tomorrow.) Checking periodically on Edward—joining him, perhaps, in a brief duet. Climbing in and out of the stroller for practice. Testing the sofa springs.

Her constant companion through all this is Dumpty, a shapeless rag doll whose best days are far behind him. About a week ago my wife put Dumpty into the washing machine, hoping at least to make him recognizable. We were not ready for the emaciated creature that emerged. Dumpty had been disemboweled during the rinse cycle. We thought that Meghan might discard this mere shell of a Dumpty. We were wrong. There was no detectable difference in her relationship with him, except that she found him easier to carry while performing her chores.

I can do my own work fairly well during most of these chores, and so I concentrate on Melville. Unfortunately, I had not counted on the arrival of the "bib-bibs." ("Bib-bibs" are birds. Again the derivation eludes me.)

"Bib-bibs, bib-bibs!" shrieks Meghan, her eyes alive with expectation. She insists that I come with her to the window. She pulls me by the hand (two fingers actually) toward the bedroom window. I see myself as a slow-wit in some Southern novel, being led oaf-like to watch the bib-bibs. And we *do* watch them. Meghan is absorbed, but as I watch them I wonder whether I parked the car under a tree last night.

Suddenly she bolts from the room (she seldom walks) and I hear her naked feet slapping against the wooden floor outside. She returns with Dumpty. She holds him up to the window, stretching him out by his pathetic, triangular arms and whispering into his non-existent ear, "Bib-bibs, Hindy, bib-bibs!" Dumpty smiles. It's a much wider smile than it used to be.

I leave them in conversation and return to my desk. Within five minutes she appears before me, wearing her mother's shoes. She reaches up to the typewriter keys and depresses four of them simultaneously.

"No, thank you, Meghan. Daddy's seen your work. He'll do it himself."

Back to the test. Determined ("Discuss illusion and reality in Benito Cereno.")

"Don't even ask, Meghan. Not today." She stands in front of me with her shoes and socks in her hand. I know the pattern. First the shoes and socks. Then the stroller. And pretty soon we're in the park. She'll want me to pick her a dandelion, or a leaf from that tree the hurricane knocked over but didn't uproot a few years ago. Oh, yes, I know the pattern.

She rests her head on my leg, just as she did when she first learned to walk. Finally she leaves, and I watch her frustration as she sits on the floor and tries for several minutes to put on one of her socks. The art proves too elusive.

She sees me looking! Back to work. ("What is the significance of the motto carved on the bow of Benito Cereno's ship?")

She pats the wicker chair, the comfortable one we sit in together to watch TV or to read, and she hastily gathers her books—*The Poky Little Puppy, the Magic Bus, The Cat in the Hat,* even that ancient copy of *National Geographic* with the penguin on the cover . . .she's got them *all.*

With her free hand, she tugs at my sleeve.

"No, Meghan," I snap irritably. "Not now. Go away and leave me alone. And take your library with you."

That does it; she leaves. She makes no further attempt to bother me. I can finish the test easily now without interference. No one trying to climb onto my lap; no extra fingers helping me type.

I see her standing quietly with her back against the sofa, tears running down her cheeks. She has two fingers of her right hand in her mouth. She holds the tragic Dumpty in her left. She watches me type, and slowly brushes the tip of Dumpty's anemic arm across her nose to comfort her.

At this moment, only for a moment, I see things as God must—in perspective, with all the pieces fitting. I see a little girl cry because I haven't time for her. Imagine ever being that important to another human being! I see the day when it won't mean so much to a tiny soul to have me sit next to her and read a story, one that means little to either of us, realizing somehow that it is the sitting next to each other that means everything. And I see the day when the frail, loyal and lovable Dumpty will vanish from the life of a little girl who has outgrown him.

I resent Dumpty for an instant. He's consoling *my girl*, and that is my concern, not his. She and I have few enough days like this to share. So the paper slips gently into the top drawer, the hood slides over the typewriter. The test will get done somehow. Tests always get done.

"Meghan, I feel like taking a walk down to the park. I was wondering if you and Edward would care to join me. I thought maybe you'd like to go on the swings for a while. Bring Dumpty—and your red sweater too. It might be windy down there."

At the word "park" the fingers leave the mouth. She laughs excitedly and begins the frantic search for her shoes and socks.

Melville will have to wait, but he won't mind. He waited most of his life for someone to discover the miracle of *Moby Dick*— and died 30 years before anyone did. No, he won't mind.

Besides, he'd understand why I must go right now—while bib-bibs still spark wonder, and before dandelions become weeds, and while a little girl thinks that a leaf from her father is a gift beyond measure.

ED BARTLEY

Most of us miss out on life's big prizes. The Pulitzer. The Nobel. Oscars. Tonys. Emmys. But we're all eligible for life's small pleasures. A pat on the back. A kiss behind the ear. A four-pound bass. A full moon. An empty parking space. A crackling fire. A great meal. A glorious sunset.

Don't fret about copping life's grand awards. Enjoy its tiny delights. There are plenty for all of us.

AUTHOR UNKNOWN

PERFECT MOMENT

Once in a lifetime there is a moment we can never forget . . .

Somewhere along the road between "beginning" and "ending" there is a perfect moment for every living soul. There may possibly be more than one. But for the most part we are too busy, too young, too adult, too sophisticated, too this or too that to recognize it—and so the moment may be lost.

My perfect moment came when I was eight years old. I awoke one spring night to find moonlight flooding my room through the open window. It was so bright that I sat up in bed. There was no sound at all anywhere. The air was soft and heavy with the fragrance of pear blossoms and honeysuckle.

I crept out of bed and tiptoed softly out of the house. Eight-year-olds were not supposed to be astir at this hour. But I wanted to sit in the swing for a while and watch the moonlight. As I closed the door behind me, I saw my mother sitting on the porch steps. She looked up and smiled and, putting her finger to her lips, reached out with her other hand and drew me down beside her. I sat as close as I could and she put her arm around me.

The whole countryside was hushed and sleeping; no lights burned in any house. The moonlight was liquid silver and so bright we could see the dark outline of the woods a mile away. "Isn't it beautiful?" I whispered, and Mother's arm tightened about me.

For a long time we were perfectly still. The stars were pale and far away. Now and then the moonlight would strike a leaf of the Maréchal Niel rose beside the porch and be caught for an instant in a dewdrop like a tiny living spark. The shrubs were hung with necklaces of diamonds, and the grass was sweet with the dampness.

In all this great brooding silence that seemed so infinite, the miracle of life was going on unseen and unheard. The bird sitting on her eggs in the mulberry tree carried out a divine purpose. The hills, undisturbed by passing centuries, proclaimed strength and grandeur. The moving of the stars, the planets, the countless worlds, all were governed and held within the safety of the omnipotent yet gentle hand of the Creator.

Mother pointed toward the cedar tree. "Look," she whispered softly, "that star seems caught in the branches."

As we watched it, suddenly from the topmost point of a pear tree a mockingbird burst into song. It was as though the joy that overflowed his heart must find expression. The notes were pure gold, free and clear and liquid as the moonlight, rising, falling, meltingly sweet. At times they were so soft as to be barely audible; then he would sing out, a rapturous *profondo*. As suddenly as it had begun, the concert ended and the night was silvery still again.

An eight-year-old does not analyze his thoughts, he may not even be aware that he is surrounded by infinity. But he sees a star impaled on the branch of a cedar tree, and knows pure ecstasy. He hears a mockingbird sing in the moonlight, and is filled with speechless joy. He feels his mother's arms about him, and knows complete security.

The surging, sweeping process of life, the moving of worlds and the flowing of tides, may be incomprehensible to him. But he may nevertheless be strangely aware that he has had a glimpse through an open door, and has known a perfect moment.

GLADYS BELL

A MOMENT CAN LAST FOREVER

"The only reality was this moment, this glistening beach and my children . . ."

Loading the car with the paraphernalia of our youngsters, ages three to nine, was hardly my idea of fun. But, precisely on schedule—and at a very early hour—I had performed that miracle. With our vacation stay on Lake Michigan now over, I hurried back into the cottage to find my wife Evie sweeping the last of the sand from the floor.

"It's six-thirty—time to leave," I said. "Where are the kids?"

Evie put away the broom. "I let them run down to the beach for one last look."

I shook my head, annoyed by this encroachment on my carefully planned schedule. Why had we bothered to rise at dawn if we weren't to get rolling before the worst of the traffic hit?

I strode across the porch and out the screen door. There, down past the rolling dunes, I spotted my four youngsters on the beach. They had discarded their shoes and were tiptoeing into the water, laughing and leaping each time a wave broke over their legs, the point obviously being to see how far into the lake they could wade without drenching their clothes. It only riled me more to realize that all their dry garments were locked, heaven knew where, in the overstuffed car trunk.

With the firmness of a master sergeant, I cupped my hands to my mouth to order my children up to the car at once. But somehow the scolding words stopped short of my lips. The sun, still low in the morning sky, etched a gold silhouette around each of the four young figures at play. For them there was left only this tiny fragment of time for draining the last drop of joy from the sun and the water and the sky.

The longer I watched, the more the scene before me assumed a magic aura, for it would never be duplicated again. What changes might we expect in our lives after the passing of another year, another ten years? The only reality was this moment, this glistening beach and these children—my children—with the sunlight trapped in their hair and the sound of their laughter mixing with the wind and the waves.

Why, I asked myself, had I been so intent on leaving at six-thirty that I had rushed from the cottage to scold them? Did I have constructive discipline in mind, or was I simply in the mood to nag because a long day's drive lay ahead? After all, there were no prizes to be won by leaving precisely on the dot. And how could I hope to maintain communication with my children, now and in later years, if I failed to keep my own youthful memory alive?

At the water's edge far below, my oldest daughter was motioning for me to join them. Then the others began waving, too, calling for Evie and me to share their fun. I hesitated for only a moment, then ran to the cottage to grab my wife's hand. Half running, half sliding down the dunes, we were soon at the beach, kicking off our shoes. With gleeful bravado we waded far out past our youngsters, Evie holding up her skirt and I my trouser cuffs, until Evie's foot slipped and she plunged squealing into the water, purposely dragging me with her.

Today, years later, my heart still warms to recall our young children's laughter that day—how full-bellied and gloriously companionable it was. And not infrequently, when they air their fondest memories, those few long-ago moments—all but denied them—are among their most precious.

GRAHAM PORTER

THE NIGHT
THE STARS FELL

One summer night in a seaside cottage, a small boy felt himself lifted from bed. Dazed with sleep, he heard his mother murmur about the lateness of the hour, heard his father laugh. Then he was borne in his father's arms, with the swiftness of a dream, down the porch steps, out onto the beach.

Overhead the sky blazed with stars. "Watch!" his father said. And incredibly, as he spoke, one of the stars moved. In a streak of golden fire, it flashed across the astonished heavens. And before the wonder of this could fade, another star leaped from its place, and then another, plunging toward the restless sea. "What is it?" the child whispered. "Shooting stars," his father said. "They come every year on certain nights in August. I thought you'd like to see the show."

That was all: just an unexpected glimpse of something haunting and mysterious and beautiful. But, back in bed, the child stared for a long time into the dark, rapt with the knowledge that all around the quiet house the night was full of the silent music of the falling stars.

Decades have passed, but I remember that night still, because I was the fortunate seven-year-old whose father believed that a new experience was more important for a small boy than an unbroken night's sleep. No doubt in my childhood I had the usual quota of playthings, but these are forgotten now. What I remember is the night the stars fell, the day we rode in a caboose, the time we tried to skin the alligator, the telegraph we made that really worked. I remember the "trophy table" in the hall where we children were encouraged to exhibit things we had found—snake skins, seashells, flowers, arrowheads, anything unusual or beautiful.

My father had, to a marvelous degree, the gift of opening doors for his children, of leading them into areas of splendid newness. This subtle art of adding dimensions to a child's world doesn't necessarily require a great deal of time. It simply involves doing things more often with our children instead of for them or to them. One woman I know keeps what she calls a "Why not?" notebook, and in it she scribbles all sorts of offbeat and fascinating proposals: "Why not take kids police head-quarters get them fingerprinted?" "Why not visit farm attempt milk cow?" "Why not arrange ride tugboat?" "Why not follow river dredge and hunt for fossilized shark's teeth?" And so they do.

One day I asked her where she got her ideas. "Oh," she said, "I don't know. But when I was a child, I had this wonderful old ne'er-do-well uncle who—" Who used to open doors for her, just as she is opening them now for her own children.

Aside from our father, we had a remarkable aunt who was a genius at suggesting spur-of-the-moment plots to blow away the dust of daily drudgeries. "Can you stand on your head?" she would ask us children. "I can!" And, tucking her skirt between her knees, she would do so. "What shall we do this afternoon?" she would cry, and answer her own question instantly: "Let's go pawn something!" Or, "There's a palm reader on the edge of town. Let's have our fortunes told!" Always a new dimension, always a magic door opening, an experience to be shared. That's the key word: we *shared*.

The easiest door to open for a child, usually, is one that leads to something you love yourself. All good teachers know this. And all good teachers know the ultimate reward: the marvel-ous moment when the spark you are breathing on bursts into a flame that henceforth will burn brightly on its own. At a United

States Golf Association tournament years ago, a pigtailed ten-year-old played creditably in the junior girls' championship. "How long have you been interested in golf?" someone asked her. "I got it for my ninth birthday," she said. "You mean your father gave you a set of clubs?" "No," she said patiently, "he gave me *golf*."

Children are naturally inquisitive and love to try new things. But they cannot find these things by themselves; someone must offer them the choices. Years ago, when the Quiz Kids were astonishing American radio audiences with their brilliance, a writer set out to discover what common denominators there were in the backgrounds of these extraordinary children. He found that some were from poor families, some from rich; some had been to superior schools, some had not.

But, in every case investigated, there was one parent, sometimes two, who shared enthusiasms with the child, who watched for areas of interest, who gave encouragement and praise for achievement, who made a game of searching out the answers to questions, who went out of his way to supply the tools of learning. No doubt the capacity for outstanding performance was already there, but it took the love and interest and companionship of a parent to bring it out.

I have a friend, a psychiatrist, who says that basically there are two types of human beings: those who think of life as a privilege and those who think of it as a problem. The first type is enthusiastic, energetic, resistant to shock, responsive to challenge. The other type is suspicious, hesitant, withholding, self-centered. To the first group, life is hopeful, exciting. To the second, it's a potential ambush. And he adds, "Tell me what sort of childhood you had and I can tell you which type you are likely to be."

The real purpose, then, of trying to open doors for children is not to divert them or amuse ourselves; it is to build eager, outgoing attitudes toward the demanding and complicated business of living. This, surely, is the most valuable legacy we can pass on to the next generation: a capacity for wonder and gratitude, a sense of aliveness and joy. Why don't we work harder at it? Probably because, as Thoreau said, our lives are frittered away in detail. Because there are times when we don't have the awareness or the selflessness or the energy.

And yet, for those of us who care what becomes of our children, the challenge is always there. None of us meets it fully, but the opportunities come again and again. Many years have passed since that night in my life when the stars fell, but the earth still turns, the sun still sets, night still sweeps over the changeless sea. And next year, when August comes with its shooting stars, *my* son will be seven.

ARTHUR GORDON

THE
BEGINNING
OF
SELF-DISCOVERY

THE ADVENTURE OF BEING ALONE

Being alone, but not lonely has rewards all its own.

I find comfort and peace in solitude. There are those who would live by the side of the road and watch the race of man go by, but my idea of a perfect place to live is a farmstead where I can't see another house. Even a distant chimney shatters my sense of tranquillity; at night, faraway lighted windows are prying eyes watching me.

You can tell a "loner" by his work: a writer who enjoys being alone writes as if talking to himself, and a painter of the same sort views landscapes without benefit of people to enliven the scene. My countryside subjects seldom have anyone there, and for a while I wondered if I had lost the knack of painting people. Presenting an art award to me, Louis Nizer brought that up, and I squirmed. "Sloane seldom has people in his paintings," he said. Then that famous lawyer with the gift of words delighted me. "But there is always someone in Sloane's paintings," he added. "It is you!"

Knowing the difference between *alone* and *lonely* can be more important than other things a student learns, and when I think of the time I spent with Latin, I wonder why the simple study of living was never considered a proper school subject.

Solitude in youth is painful because the art of living comfortably with it has not yet been learned; it is usually only in maturity that solitude becomes delicious. At one time, when life was confusing and my mind lacked decision, I went to people for advice. I have since learned that the answers were usually within me all the while. Now when I am perplexed, I seek seclusion and, in the eloquence of silence, I wait for the replies to arrive. And they do.

I was introduced to being alone at an early stage. Having run away from home to work on a remote Pennsylvania farm with Hans and Hilda Appelbaum, I knew well what it meant to be homesick; they spoke only German and I knew little of their language. After supper we would sit on the porch and listen to the sounds of summer and make vague attempts at conversation. One night Hilda noted the droning of an insect known thereabouts as the lonesome bug. *"Was ist das?"* she asked.

I tried to act out the word "lonesome." I feigned tears, looked forlorn and uttered what I thought were lonesome sounds. She got the point. *"Ach!"* she exclaimed. *"Das ist ein heimweh* (homesick) *bugg!"* I will always remember trying to explain to Hans and Hilda that being alone was some sort of disaster. Now, at my age, to mimic solitude I would smile and look contented.

As you walk along a crowded street, you usually pass people without a glance, but on a quiet street when you approach a solitary person, you find yourself nodding, even saying hello. I recall hiking across a prairie and seeing someone nearly a mile off heading roughly in my direction. A quarter mile off, we both felt called upon to head closer, wave a greeting, and approach each other. We introduced ourselves, chatted and then continued separately on our way. It was a strange performance provoked by the unexplainable magnetism of two people being alone.

The writer—a hermit in the cave of his mind—is often a lonely person. But loneliness can also be a sweet suffering; and suffering, so they say, makes one more sincere. Such a sincere writer was Van Wyck Brooks, who knew New England well. He once asked me if I enjoyed my move from the city and I told him how the country produced a strange loneliness that I actually enjoyed.

"That," he said, "makes you old-school American. Loneliness is particularly evident on the New England face; it is the American bittersweet of pain and pleasure. But those who live understandingly with it," he added, "find a tolerable and even exciting companion."

I knew what he meant. I have since enjoyed that rambling melancholy of deserted farms and stone-fence monuments of other days. In the most stirring landscape, I still sense a pleasant echo of nostalgic contemplation.

ERIC SLOANE

A man must keep a little back shop where he can be himself without reserve. In solitude alone can he know true freedom.
MICHEL EYQUEM DE MONTAIGNE

MEANING
FOR MY DAYS

Solitude can lead to the joy of self-discovery.

From birth to middle age—for more than 40 years—I lived in the enclosure of family. I grew up in one family. I raised another. Family was the center upon which turned my days, thoughts and wishes. But then time and circumstance converged, and change fell upon me.

My father died. My marriage ended in divorce. My mother turned fragile and smiled in confusion when I kissed her. My three children were grown, ranging ever outward, as I approached what I had never before imagined: a life alone.

There came a morning leaden with finality: my last in the house that had sheltered so much of family. I touched the walls in farewell, feeling a gathering of ghosts, a tender grief that spanned my whole history. I recalled the long-ago bright energies of my parents, the sweet hopefulness of my marriage begun. I saw babies trudging belly-first dragging toys on strings, and heard shouts of children from the meadow. I wept for birthdays, Christmas feasts, and ordinary suppers set for five.

And then I followed the mover's van into the next village to a tiny apartment that stunned me with unfamiliarity. At dusk, bone-weary, I sat in the unpeopled quiet and suffered from the knowledge that I might be alone for the rest of my life.

I had children and friends upon whom I could depend, to be sure. But I realized that unless I could become my own best resource, I would never get over the fears that filled me.

Aloud, to be certain I heard it, I said, *Now everything is up to me.* I resolved that somehow I would take responsibility for my own health and wealth and happiness. I'd make my own connections with the world and find meaning for my days.

At first just getting by seemed difficult. Why? I was a grown woman. Why did it seem I was learning everything for the first time?

Dismayed and yet determined, I hammered my thumb blue—but I hung the shelves. I confronted the trapped mouse thrashing about in the cupboard. I studied the language of tax forms. And when anyone asked, "How are you?" I said, "*Fine!*" Slowly I felt surer; then, heady. I celebrated every success with "Look at me! I did it!"

I'd gone through life believing in the strength and competence of others; never in my own. Now, dazzled, I discovered that my capacities were real. It was like finding a fortune in the lining of an old coat.

There were still painful times. But there was an advantage to aloneness: the space around me admitted light, illuminating perspectives I'd never glimpsed in the midst of family. I began to understand that the world had more in it than I'd perceived before. I saw before me a profusion of choices; more ways to think and feel and be and do than I had ever contemplated.

I suppose I've read a thousand explanations of happiness. I have my own: When I experience something I care about—a shining day, a gentle silence between friends—happiness comes of itself. Therefore, I decided, happiness begins in caring; in me. Caring arises from within, as love does, moves outward, and joins with life. That's what I wanted—that joining.

I felt an enormous rush of optimism. I knew that I cared about a great many things, and I knew what they were. If I cared enough, life would gain meaning. I cared especially about people. Nothing else had ever, for me, approached the significance of the lives that were part of my life.

I cared about knowing and being known. Feelings, dreams, deeds, depths and secrets mattered. The touch of a hand, the weight of a baby, the power of a glance. Even writing was, for me, a means to reach out to others.

I can have all that, I thought, and felt immensely better. I could go on, as always, finding and cherishing and being with people. My children, for all their independence, were not lost to me. We'd reached a new level of generous delight at seeing one another grow up—each separate, but still family. I could even include myself among those I cared about. I'd learned to value my own company. Thus, a durable calm, a trust in myself and in life, settled where anxiety had been.

Looking for a chance to be useful, I volunteered to keep records for a mental-health service headquartered across the street. I became so involved that soon the staff trained me to work in therapy. In time I was invited to conferences of professionals in the next town, the next state, and then—the first great journey of my life!—England and Wales.

"Cross the street and see the world!" I marveled.

My horizons expanded steadily as I risked other opportunities and experiments. But it was at home that I assimilated my experience and counted my most immediate blessings. I found peace and comfort. Life worked. For me, my daughter and my two sons.

I remember a night when all four of us, in rare reunion, stayed late talking. I lingered awake afterward, reflecting upon the breadth of my children's adult visions; their capacities to care for others, and for themselves; their sturdy souls; their compassion.

Would they marry? Have children? They were better prepared for either than I had been. With rue I thought, *I have lived my life in the wrong order.*

But that regret is gone now. There is more to me than what I've made of these years alone. I'm shaped by everything I've ever known or done. Child I was, and wife, and mother; as educated by the babies I rocked as by my mother's presence, my father's voice, my husband's resilient optimism.

Now I have learned the lessons of solitude—no doubt imperfectly, but nevertheless with profit. I hold it precious to know that I am not, even here, *alone*. I am a belonger in a world of infinite possibility, where happiness can be the earned reward of caring.

JOAN MILLS

Self-respect cannot be hunted. It cannot be purchased. It is never for sale. It cannot be fabricated out of public relations. It comes to us when we are alone, in quiet moments, in quiet places, when we suddenly realize that, knowing the good, we have done it; knowing the beautiful, we have served it; knowing the truth, we have spoken it.

A. WHITNEY GRISWOLD

"I WANTED TO DO IT ALL"

Explorer/adventurer John Goddard has been everywhere, done everything. But of all the worlds he has conquered, the most challenging has been the world within.

Forty-five years ago, John Goddard drew up a list of everything he wanted to accomplish in his life. He was just 15, a kid in the suburban confines of Los Angeles. But even then he had dreams of faraway lands and a vision of himself as a great explorer. He titled his paper "My Life List."

"Explore the Nile, Amazon and Congo rivers," he wrote. "Climb Mount Everest, Mount Kilimanjaro, the Matterhorn. Ride an elephant, camel, ostrich and bronco. Retrace the travels of Marco Polo and Alexander the Great. Appear in a Tarzan movie. Land on and take off from an aircraft carrier. Read the works of Shakespeare, Plato and Aristotle. Compose a work of music. Write a book. Visit every country in the world. Marry and have children. Visit the moon."

He numbered each item, and when he finished he had 127 goals. The list was not simply a rainy afternoon's daydreaming: it was a challenge.

Today a trim, youthful-looking 60, Goddard is a veteran of countless safaris and expeditions, a filmmaker, author and lecturer. He still makes his home in Southern California, living with his wife in a conventional ranch-style house. Inside, though, he sits easily amid the shrunken heads, silver daggers, bright weavings and other exotic artifacts that recall his many adventures. When that long-ago list is mentioned, Goddard has a soft smile for his younger self.

"I wrote the list," he explains, "because at fifteen I was very aware of my limitations. I was just an unformed human who had potential like everyone else, and I really wanted to do something with my life. I set up a blueprint of goals so that I would always have something to work for. I was also aware of people around me who had gotten into ruts, had never taken risks, never challenged themselves in any way. I was determined not to go that route."

With his dreams formally on paper, Goddard lost no time in turning them into reality. By age 16 he had explored the Okefenokee Swamp in Georgia and the Everglades in Florida with his father. "That was one of the first things I accomplished on my list," he remembers. "That and learning to skindive, owning a horse and driving a tractor." By 20 he had dived in the Caribbean, Aegean and Red seas. He had also become an Air Force flier and flown 33 combat missions over Europe.

By age 21 he had traveled in 21 countries, and shortly after turning 22 he discovered a Mayan temple deep in the jungles of Guatemala. That same year he became the youngest member ever admitted to the Adventurer's Club of Los Angeles, and he began planning his most ambitious quest, goal No. 1: exploring the Nile River.

Goddard was 26 when he arrived at the source of the Nile in the mountains of Burundi with his two expedition partners, Frenchmen André Davy and Jean La Porte. La Porte was the only one with kayaking experience. "All the government officials told us it would be impossible for three men in little sixty-pound kayaks to go the whole, four-thousand-mile length of the river," Goddard recalls. "But their naysaying only made us more determined."

The trio suffered hippo attacks, bouts with malaria, blinding sandstorms, miles of dangerous rapids and a chase by rifle-shooting river bandits. But ten months after they had set out, the three "Niloteers," as they called themselves, paddled triumphantly from the mouth of the Nile into the blue of the Mediterranean.

"I learned so much about myself on that trip," says Goddard, "about the exhilaration of succeeding, about living life fully and intensely. It gave me extra impetus to go after my other goals. If we'd thought ahead to all the miles and problems we faced, we probably never would have left the tent. But by taking each day at a time, we eventually reached our goal. And I think that is the way to approach life—in small increments, cramming them with as much activity, learning, love and friendship as possible."

Following the Nile expedition, Goddard began checking off his other goals in quick succession: he rafted the entire length of the Colorado River in 1954; explored all of the 2700-mile Congo River in 1956; lived with headhunters and cannibals in the wilds of South America, Borneo and New Guinea; climbed Mount Ararat and Mount Kilimanjaro; flew jet fighters at twice the speed of sound; wrote a book (*Kayaks Down the Nile*); married and had five children. After starting out as a full-time anthropologist, he launched a career as a film-maker and lecturer, and in ensuing years has financed his expeditions through his talks and films.

To date, Goddard has completed 107 of his 127 goals. He has received the honors due an explorer, including memberships in the Royal Geographical Society of England and the New York Explorers Club. And he has had 38 close encounters with death while pursuing his goals. "These experiences have taught me to value life more deeply and savor everything I can," he says. "People often go through life never knowing what it is to express great courage, strength or endurance. But I've found that when you think you're certain to die, you suddenly find an untapped well of power and control you didn't dream you possessed. When you express that, it's like elevating your soul to another dimension."

Although Goddard believes in accomplishment, he doesn't

feel compelled to complete every item on his list. "It is simply a guideline. It does not control my life," he says. Still, he manages to check off a new item almost every year, and constantly sets additional goals and challenges for himself. "I try to assess my life, see what areas I could improve emotionally, intellectually, physically." He believes that such annual evaluations lead to more productivity and to deeper happiness.

"It's helpful to look at your life and ask: 'If I had one more year to live, what would I do?' We all have things we want to achieve. Don't put them off—do them now!"

Goddard has no shortage of future projects, including an ascent of Mount McKinley (item No. 23). He has never let go of any of his goals. "That way, when the opportunity presents itself, I'm ready." And yes, in his heart of hearts, he firmly believes that one day he will even achieve item No. 125: "Visit the moon."

VIRGINIA MORELL

I once had a friend whose ambition in life was to acquire experiences worth owning. His argument was that they constitute the only real wealth in this world. An experience that is really worth having and owning, he would point out, does not have to be insured. It is never subject to any tax, and your executor will never have to account for it. And your heirs will relish their recollection of your tale of it.

Such an experience, he used to say, was about the only thing a man could acquire that someone else did not have some kind of stake in. Such experiences are really your own—to have and to hold for keeps. A man can relive them in his mind all his life.

DUDLEY CAMMETT LUNT

The most glorious moments in your life are not the so-called days of success, but rather those days when out of dejection and despair you feel rise in you a challenge to life, and the promise of future accomplishments.

GUSTAVE FLAUBERT

A WALK ACROSS AMERICA

A young man's remarkable 4751-mile odyssey, from disillusionment to the discovery of what life in this country is all about.

It was so hot, I felt I was going to melt into the pavement. We had been heading down Alabama country road 117 at our customary speed: three miles an hour. We means my dog, Cooper-Half-Malamute, and myself. Then I saw a country store, a quivering shape in the heat haze. Dumping my backpack against a tree, I rushed past a blue-overalled farmer drinking a Dr. Pepper, and burst through the door. I grabbed everything cold and wet in sight and started drinking.

Dropping payment on the counter, I plunged back into that Alabama heat. As I hosed Cooper with icy water and let him lap to his heart's content, the farmer finally spoke: "Where y'all started to?"

"Well, sir, my dog, Cooper, and I, we happen to be walking across America." And then I answered all the down-home questions that I'd been asked in the previous nine months. How I'd started this walk across America on October 15, 1973, in upper New York State from the college town of Alfred, where I'd gotten my Bachelor of Fine Arts in sculpture and ceramics the June before. How I was born and raised in Greenwich, Conn.

Then he came to the question they always asked: "Now, son, I don't aim to be nosy, but *why* would a young college feller like y'self go out and walk across the country?"

"Well, I decided I'd take a look at America firsthand, to see if what I'd read and heard about it was true." I had grown up in the late 1960s and early '70s, when my country seemed to be pulling loose from its moorings with student protests, peace marches, Kent State, racial violence, Watergate. Like many of my friends, I was confused. And so this walk of mine amounted, in my mind, to giving the country another chance.

"I've come to realize what a bad press America's been giving itself. There's a lot of good that also needs telling. I haven't gone a day that someone hasn't been kind, or helpful or thoughtful. Ordinary folks they may be, but they're heroes to me."

He smiled. "Welcome to Alabama, boy! You just throw your pack and that there wolf in my pickup, and you can put down at my place for the night."

"Sorry," I said. "But I promised myself when I began that I would walk, really *walk*, every step of the way while I'm traveling."

"Well, you got to camp somewheres," he said. "Down the road a spell you'll see a pecan orchard. Plop down there if you like. May God bless you and your dog on your walk. My wife and I will put you both in our prayers."

He drove off. I realized I hadn't even asked him his name. And I realized, too, that I had just met another American hero.

Cooper and I hit the early-evening, meditative country road to that pecan orchard. Watching him rocket after a mysterious rustle, I remembered how he and I had trained for this walk for 4½ months, running hundreds of hours and turning our suburbanized muscles into the catgut and piano wire you need, man or dog, if you're going to walk 20, 30, 40 miles a day for months on end.

From the start, I decided I would not become mileage crazy. I wanted to share every environment I passed through with the people who were rooted in it. My plan was to take nine months or so to make a rough V across the United States—from Alfred to the Gulf Coast, then over to the Pacific—maybe 5000 miles in all. When practical, we would go by the wilds and back roads.

The day we left, a crowd of friends saw Cooper and me off as we stepped into that Allegheny autumn morning. We hiked 30 miles to our first night's camp in the northern Pennsylvania mountains. Fast as we walked, we were no match for the great flocks of migrating geese overhead.

Homer Davenport lives all alone on a mountaintop 12 miles north of Saltville, Va. Anyone in these parts will tell you he is the greatest living American mountain man. People said I had to meet him.

So I went. Homer's front sidewalk is a rocky stream, and there I found him—looking for all the world like a prophet on a holy mountain, an ageless old man with white shoulder-length hair.

In his cabin of logs and scrap, we warmed our hands by the fire. Then Homer whipped up hot corn bread, applesauce, and home-grown yellow beets the size of cantaloupes. I never ate a more satisfying meal. We talked until 3 a.m., exchanging details of our lives like two collectors trading rare old coins. I slept on ashwood shavings from the ax handles Homer carves as a sideline.

"Maybe when you finish walkin'," he said, "maybe then you'll come back. This mountaintop'll always be here, even if I ain't."

I'll never forget his blue mountain eyes looking clear through me as he spoke, or the warm sandpapery feel of his hand as we said good-by.

I headed into the northeast corner of Alabama—where I met the blue-overalled farmer with the Dr. Pepper—then crossed into Tennessee.

On October 16, tragedy struck: Cooper was run over by a

truck. His death left me stunned and despondent. I laid him into freshly dug soil, expecting him somehow to burst out of the confining earth. As I headed south, I had never been so alone.

Nurturing vague fears of what the Alabama "rednecks" I'd heard about might do to a bearded Connecticut Yankee, I walked through tiny, tenacious towns like Wren and Arley and Sipsey and Graysville, then on to Montgomery and the Alabama capitol. I said I wanted to talk to the governor. Even though I'd been told you could do that, I expected a big hassle. To my amazement, there was none. Sitting in his wheelchair, a smiling George C. Wallace held out a firm hand. I explained what I was about on this walk of mine, how all my stereotype notions of southern rednecks had been discarded. He grinned.

"Well, Peter," he said, "with that red beard and sunburned skin of yours, you qualify as something of a redneck yourself."

And so I reached the Gulf Coast. I particularly loved the sea air, filled with soul-stirring vapors. After all the land-locked miles I had walked, the 13 pairs of shoes I'd gone through, it was pure poetry to go barefoot at the water's foamy edge.

Facing New Orleans, I quickened my steps. I remembered Bill Hanks, whom I'd met at a revival meeting in Mobile. At the time a graduate student at the New Orleans Baptist Theological Seminary, Bill had invited me to visit him, and soon I found myself—backpack, sweaty duds, leaky shoes and all—on the elegant campus.

One night out strolling, I heard laughter explode from a plantation-like mansion that housed the few female students on campus. I was drawn inside—and barged right into a water war! She was there, poised, a tall girl with a jug of water in her hands. She wore jeans, and her hair was thick and curly black. Smiling angelically, she dumped the water over me. I knew in Barbara Pennell I had met my match.

Everything was perfect that first date as we drove around the French Quarter—as it was in the days after. And soon we decided to get married. We had no honeymoon. A job on an oil rig came through, and for four months I worked as a galley hand and roustabout on the *J Storm I,* 44 feet above the Gulf.

When we had enough money to start walking, we concentrated on hardening our bodies. It was taxing for Barbara, who'd never camped out in her life, but she had the inner toughness of pioneer ancestors who had trekked to Missouri in covered wagons. By July 5, 1976, we were ready to start for the Pacific.

By first light we ferried across the brown Mississippi and headed out. The temperature was nearly 100. We walked 12 miles the first day, then 15, then 16. Barbara's feet turned into masses of blisters. She wept but kept going.

We entered the wide, wide world of Texas, with red cattle as big as Chevy pickups. September sizzled. We slowed down a bit and even stayed overnight at a motel every week or two. But higher expenses drained our meager finances. By the time we were at the outskirts of Dallas, we were down to $1.87.

We didn't know a soul. Ahead, the steel-and-glass skyline grew like a geometric cactus out of the flat, bare plains. The winds whirled around us; we felt lonely and scared.

We joined hands and prayed, and then kept going. Less than an hour later, Ron Hall came riding up. "You folks hungry?" he asked. Turned out he was the minister of a small church. He took us into Dallas, where we ate our fill at El Chico, a restaurant run by a family named Cuellar. It was my first real Mexican meal, and my stomach told me this was the place to get a job. We wintered over in Dallas, and I worked my way up from bus-boy to waiter.

When time came to leave in spring 1977, I had to boil off all those tamales in a month of conditioning. Then we moved into the West Texas world of dust storms, tornadoes, cactus, melting roads, rattlesnakes and fire ants. After I'd worked more than a month in the Panhandle, cleaning out gas wells near Borger, we finally made it to New Mexico.

When I think about Idaho, I think about the W. T. Williams ranch, where you can ride a good saddle horse all day and not see another human being—just sagebrush, howling coyotes, fence posts, a few golden eagles and scattered herds of cattle. I hired on there. For two months I wrestled 375-pound calves and helped harvest corn, wheat, hay and pinto beans.

In Oregon we encountered desolate ranchland, blizzards, and 100-mile spaces between towns. Barbara grew depressed, and talked about letting me go on without her.

We were walking through the coldest winter here since 1919. When Barbara grew weaker, too tired even to move out of the way of the spray from the passing logging trucks, we visited a doctor. "Son," he told me, "you're going to be a father." I started jumping and hollering. Barbara was radiant.

Understanding what her symptoms meant, she found the strength and will to go on. After a week more of sub-zero temperatures and howling snows, we reached the spine of the Cascades. Nothing was going to stop the *three* of us. We coasted down to the Oregon lowlands. We could smell the Pacific!

We walked our final mile on January 18, 1979. We'd stopped in Florence, Ore., so our families and some of the friends we'd met over the past five years and 4751 miles could join us for the final steps. As we approached the ocean's foaming surf, Barbara and I kept on walking, right up to our waists. Everyone was yelling, laughing, crying and hugging each other. Especially Barbara and me.

We'd done what we set out to do—and much more. I had found the love of my life, and I had found America. I had lived and walked through 17 states and encountered countless kinds of life-styles and all kinds of people. When I was lonely, cold, hungry, tired, hot, dirty and often without money, caring people took me into their homes and hearts, not just once, but time and time again. These American people helped to change my attitudes about America, patriotism, love and God. I used to think that anyone who talked about honor or courage or America with affection was a hypocrite. Now, such words are alive for me, fitting together like notes of an inspired song that I will hear forever.

PETER JENKINS

ACKNOWLEDGMENTS

"One Step to Excitement" ("One Step to Adventure") by Elizabeth Starr Hill. Christian Herald, September 1965. © 1965 by Christian Herald Assn., Inc.; excerpt from *Viva Mexico* by Charles McComb Flandrau (Harper); "Dare to Make Mistakes" by Beth Day. © 1967 by The Reader's Digest Assn., Inc.; "Take That Chance!" by Frank Harvey. Kansas City Star, July 1976. © 1976 by The Kansas City Star Co.; "Dig Into the World" by Alan Alda. Connecticut College News, Summer 1980. © 1980 by Alan Alda; excerpt from *Unfinished Business* by Dr. Halford E. Luccock. Reprinted with permission of Harper & Row, Publishers, Inc.; "The Grammar of Life" by William Wallace Rose. The Ithaca Journal, July 1957. © 1957 by The Ithaca Journal; "Words of Wisdom from Dr. Seuss" by Theodor Seuss Geisel. © 1977 by Theodor Seuss Geisel; "The Magic of Enthusiasm" ("Secret of Enthusiasm") by Michael Drury. Glamour, July 1960. © 1960 by Michael Drury; "Secrets of the Soaring Spirit" ("Give Yourself a Lift") by Hilton Gregory. © 1975 by The Reader's Digest Assn., Inc.; Mary Meek Atkeson; "The Awesome Power to Be Ourselves" by Ardis Whitman. © 1983 by The Reader's Digest Assn., Inc.; excerpt from an article about Dr. Eric Berne by Jack Fincher. Life, August 1966. © 1966 by Time Inc. Reprinted with permission; "Make Your Dreams Come True" from *Positive Imaging* by Norman Vincent Peale. © 1982 by NVP F.H.R.C.; excerpt from *The Shape of a Year* by Jean Hersey (Scribner). © 1977 by Jean Hersey; "Seven Secrets of Peak Performance" by Morton Hunt. © 1982 by The Reader's Digest Assn., Inc.; "Overtaken by Joy" by Ardis Whitman. © 1965 by The Reader's Digest Assn., Inc.; Storm Jameson, This Week Magazine, May 1966. © 1966 by Storm Jameson. "Do Clouds Sleep?" from *Elephant Bones & Lonelyhearts* by Ronald Rood (Stephen Greene Press). © 1977 by Ronald Rood; excerpt from *The Age of Triumph and Frustration* by Charles Yost. © 1964 by Robert Speller & Sons, Publishers, Inc.; "Now . . . While There's Time" by Ed Bartley. © 1969 by The Reader's Digest Assn., Inc.; United Technologies Corporation; "Perfect Moment" by Gladys Bell. © 1977 by The Reader's Digest Assn., Inc.;

Designed by Patrice Barrett

Illustrations by Cris Muscott

Typeset in Optima